PLAYS
A PHOENIX TOO FREQUENT
THOR, WITH ANGELS
THE LADY'S NOT FOR BURNING

CHRISTOPHER FRY

PLAYS

A Phoenix Too Frequent

Thor, With Angels

The Lady's Not For Burning

OXFORD UNIVERSITY PRESS

OXFORD NEW YORK

Oxford University Press, Walton Street, Oxford OX2 6DP

London Glasgow New York Toronto
Delhi Bombay Calcutta Madras Karachi
Kuala Lumpur Singapore Hong Kong Tokyo
Nairobi Dar es Salaam Cape Town
Melbourne Wellington
and associate companies in
Beirut Berlin Ibadan Mexico City

ISBN 0 19 281056 1

© Copyright 1948, 1949, 1950, 1973 by Christopher Fry

A Phoenix Too Frequent first published by Hollis & Carter 1946. Reissued by Oxford University Press, London, 1949

Thor, With Angels first published in an acting edition by H. J. Goulden Ltd., 1948. First published by Oxford University Press, London, 1949

The Lady's Not for Burning first published by Oxford University Press, London, 1949. Second edition 1950, revised 1973

The three plays first published as an Oxford University Press paperback 1969 and reprinted 1973, 1974, 1977, 1978, 1982

Printed in Great Britain by
The Thetford Press Ltd.
Thetford, Norfolk

CONTENTS

A PHOENIX TOO FREQUENT

A Comedy

To
MY WIFE

A PHOENIX TOO FREQUENT

First produced at the Mercury Theatre, London
25 April 1946

Dynamene	.	. HERMIONE HANNEN
Doto	. .	ELEANOR SUMMERFIELD
Tegeus-Chromis	.	ALAN WHEATLEY

Directed by E. Martin Browne

Revived at the Arts Theatre, London
20 November 1946

Dynamene	.	HERMIONE HANNEN
Doto	. .	. . JOAN WHITE
Tegeus-Chromis	.	PAUL SCOFIELD

Directed by Noël Willman

CHARACTERS

DYNAMENE

DOTO

TEGEUS-CHROMIS

SCENE

The tomb of Virilius, near Ephesus; night

NOTE

*The story was got from Jeremy Taylor who
had it from Petronius*

'To whom conferr'd a peacock's indecent,
A squirrel's harsh, a phoenix too frequent.'

Robert Burton quoting Martial

An underground tomb, in darkness except for the very low light of an oil-lamp. Above ground the starlight shows a line of trees on which hang the bodies of several men. It also penetrates a gate and falls on to the first of the steps which descend into the darkness of the tomb. DOTO *talks to herself in the dark.*

DOTO. Nothing but the harmless day gone into black
Is all the dark is. And so what's my trouble?
Demons is so much wind. Are so much wind.
I've plenty to fill my thoughts. All that I ask
Is don't keep turning men over in my mind,
Venerable Aphrodite. I've had my last one
And thank you. I thank thee. He smelt of sour grass
And was likeable. He collected ebony quoits.

                                [An owl hoots near at hand.
O Zeus! O some god or other, where is the oil?
Fire's from Prometheus. I thank thee. If I
Mean to die I'd better see what I'm doing.
            *[She fills the lamp with oil. The flame burns up brightly and
            shows* DYNAMENE, *beautiful and young, leaning asleep
            beside a bier.*
Honestly, I would rather have to sleep
With a bald bee-keeper who was wearing his boots
Than spend more days fasting and thirsting and crying
In a tomb. I shouldn't have said that. Pretend
I didn't hear myself. But life and death
Is cat and dog in this double-bed of a world.
My master, my poor master, was a man
Whose nose was as straight as a little buttress,

7

And now he has taken it into Elysium
Where it won't be noticed among all the other straightness.
                    [*The owl cries again and wakens* DYNAMENE.
Oh, them owls. Those owls. It's woken her.

DYNAMENE. Ah! I'm breathless. I caught up with the ship
But it spread its wings, creaking a cry of *Dew*,
Dew! and flew figurehead foremost into the sun.

DOTO. How crazy, madam.

DYNAMENE.   Doto, draw back the curtains.
I'll take my barley-water.

DOTO.   We're not at home
Now, madam. It's the master's tomb.

DYNAMENE.   Of course!
Oh, I'm wretched. Already I have disfigured
My vigil. My cynical eyelids have soon dropped me
In a dream.

DOTO.   But then it's possible, madam, you might
Find yourself in bed with him again
In a dream, madam. Was he on the ship?

DYNAMENE. He was the ship.

DOTO.   Oh. That makes it different.

DYNAMENE. He was the ship. He had such a deck, Doto,
Such a white, scrubbed deck. Such a stern prow,
Such a proud stern, so slim from port to starboard.
If ever you meet a man with such fine masts
Give your life to him, Doto. The figurehead
Bore his own features, so serene in the brow
And hung with a little seaweed. O Virilius,
My husband, you have left a wake in my soul.
You cut the glassy water with a diamond keel.
I must cry again.

DOTO.   What, when you mean to join him?
Don't you believe he will be glad to see you, madam?
Thankful to see you, I should imagine, among
Them shapes and shades; all shapes of shapes and all
Shades of shades, from what I've heard. I know
I shall feel odd at first with Cerberus,
Sop or no sop. Still, I know how you feel, madam.
You think he may find a temptation in Hades.
I shouldn't worry. It would help him to settle down.

> [DYNAMENE *weeps.*

It would only be *fun*, madam. He couldn't go far
With a shade.

DYNAMENE.   He was one of the coming men.
He was certain to have become the most well-organized provost
The town has known, once they had made him provost.
He was so punctual, you could regulate
The sun by him. He made the world succumb
To his daily revolution of habit. But who,
In the world he has gone to, will appreciate that?
O poor Virilius! To be a coming man
Already gone—it must be distraction.
Why did you leave me walking about our ambitions
Like a cat in the ruins of a house? Promising husband,
Why did you insult me by dying? Virilius,
Now I keep no flower, except in the vase
Of the tomb.

DOTO.   O poor madam! O poor master!
I presume so far as to cry somewhat for myself
As well. I know you won't mind, madam. It's two
Days not eating makes me think of my uncle's
Shop in the country, where he has a hardware business,
Basins, pots, ewers, and alabaster birds.

He makes you die of laughing. O madam,
Isn't it sad?

[*They both weep.*

DYNAMENE.   How could I have allowed you
To come and die of my grief? Doto, it puts
A terrible responsibility on me. Have you
No grief of your own you could die of?

DOTO.   Not really, madam.

DYNAMENE. Nothing?

DOTO.   Not really. They was all one to me.
Well, all but two was all one to me. And they,
Strange enough, was two who kept recurring.
I could never be sure if they had gone for good
Or not; and so that kept things cheerful, madam.
One always gave a wink before he deserted me,
The other slapped me as it were behind, madam;
Then they would be away for some months.

DYNAMENE.   Oh Doto,
What an unhappy life you were having to lead.

DOTO. Yes, I'm sure. But never mind, madam,
It seemed quite lively then. And now I know
It's what you say; life is more big than a bed
And full of miracles and mysteries like
One man made for one woman, etcetera, etcetera.
Lovely. I feel sung, madam, by a baritone
In mixed company with everyone pleased.
And so I had to come with you here, madam,
For the last sad chorus of me. It's all
Fresh to me. Death's a new interest in life,
If it doesn't disturb you, madam, to have me crying.

It's because of us not having breakfast again.
And the master, of course. And the beautiful world.
And you crying too, madam. Oh—Oh!

DYNAMENE. I can't forbid your crying; but you must cry
On the other side of the tomb. I'm becoming confused.
This is my personal grief and my sacrifice
Of self, solus. Right over there, darling girl.

DOTO. What here?

DYNAMENE.   Now, if you wish, you may cry, Doto.
But our tears are very different. For me
The world is all with Charon, all, all,
Even the metal and plume of the rose garden,
And the forest where the sea fumes overhead
In vegetable tides, and particularly
The entrance to the warm baths in Arcite Street
Where we first met;—all!—the sun itself
Trails an evening hand in the sultry river
Far away down by Acheron. I am lonely,
Virilius. Where is the punctual eye
And where is the cautious voice which made
Balance-sheets sound like Homer and Homer sound
Like balance-sheets? The precision of limbs, the amiable
Laugh, the exact festivity? Gone from the world.
You were the peroration of nature, Virilius.
You explained everything to me, even the extremely
Complicated gods. You wrote them down
In seventy columns. Dear curling calligraphy!
Gone from the world, once and for all. And I taught you
In your perceptive moments to appreciate me.
You said I was harmonious, Virilius,
Moulded and harmonious, little matronal

Ox-eye, your package. And then I would walk
Up and down largely, as it were making my own
Sunlight. What a mad blacksmith creation is
Who blows his furnaces until the stars fly upward
And iron Time is hot and politicians glow
And bulbs and roots sizzle into hyacinth
And orchis, and the sand puts out the lion,
Roaring yellow, and oceans bud with porpoises,
Blenny, tunny and the almost unexisting
Blindfish; throats are cut, the masterpiece
Looms out of labour; nations and rebellions
Are spat out to hang on the wind—and all is gone
In one Virilius, wearing his office tunic,
Checking the pence column as he went.
Where's animation now? What is there that stays
To dance? The eye of the one-eyed world is out.

                                                    [*She weeps.*

DOTO. I shall try to grieve a little, too.
It would take lessons, I imagine, to do it out loud
For long. If I could only remember
Any one of those fellows without wanting to laugh.
Hopeless, I am. Now those good pair of shoes
I gave away without thinking, that's a different—
Well, I've cried enough about *them*, I suppose.
Poor madam, poor master.

            [TEGEUS *comes through the gate to the top of the steps.*

TEGEUS.   What's your trouble?

DOTO.   Oh!
Oh! Oh, a man. I thought for a moment it was something
With harm in it. Trust a man to be where it's dark.
What is it? Can't you sleep?

TEGEUS.   Now, listen—

DOTO.   Hush!
Remember you're in the grave. You must go away.
Madam is occupied.

TEGEUS.   What, here?

DOTO.   Becoming
Dead. We both are.

TEGEUS.   What's going on here?

DOTO.   Grief.
Are you satisfied now?

TEGEUS.   Less and less. Do you know
What the time is?

DOTO.   I'm not interested.
We've done with all that. Go away. Be a gentleman.
If we can't be free of men in a grave
Death's a dead loss.

TEGEUS.   It's two in the morning. All
I ask is what are women doing down here
At two in the morning?

DOTO.   Can't you see she's crying?
Or is she sleeping again? Either way
She's making arrangements to join her husband.

TEGEUS.   Where?

DOTO. Good god, in the Underworld, dear man. Haven't you
  learnt
About life and death?

TEGEUS.   In a manner, yes; in a manner;
The rudiments. So the lady means to die?

DOTO. For love; beautiful, curious madam.

TEGEUS.   Not curious;
I've had thoughts like it. Death is a kind of love.
Not anything I can explain.

DOTO.   You'd better come in
And sit down.

TEGEUS.   I'd be grateful.

DOTO.   Do. It will be my last
Chance to have company, in the flesh.

TEGEUS.   Do you mean
You're going too?

DOTO.   Oh, certainly I am.
Not anything I can explain.
It all started with madam saying a man
Was two men really, and I'd only noticed one,
One each, I mean. It seems he has a soul
As well as his other troubles. And I like to know
What I'm getting with a man. I'm inquisitive,
I suppose you'd call me.

TEGEUS.   It takes some courage.

DOTO.   Well, yes
And no. I'm fond of change.

TEGEUS.   Would you object
To have me eating my supper here?

DOTO.   Be careful
Of the crumbs. We don't want a lot of squeaking mice
Just when we're dying.

TEGEUS.   What a sigh she gave then.
Down the air like a slow comet.
And now she's all dark again. Mother of me.
How long has this been going on?

DOTO.   Two days.
It should have been three by now, but at first
Madam had difficulty with the Town Council. They said
They couldn't have a tomb used as a private residence.
But madam told them she wouldn't be eating here,
Only suffering, and they thought that would be all right.

TEGEUS. Two of you. Marvellous. Who would have said
I should ever have stumbled on anything like this?
Do you have to cry? Yes, I suppose so. It's all
Quite reasonable.

DOTO.   Your supper and your knees.
That's what's making me cry. I can't bear sympathy
And they're sympathetic.

TEGEUS.   Please eat a bit of something.
I've no appetite left.

DOTO.   And see her go ahead of me?
Wrap it up; put it away. You sex of wicked beards!
It's no wonder you have to shave off your black souls
Every day as they push through your chins.
I'll turn my back on you. It means utter
Contempt. Eat? Utter contempt. Oh, little new rolls!

TEGEUS. Forget it, forget it; please forget it. Remember
I've had no experience of this kind of thing before.
Indeed I'm as sorry as I know how to be. Ssh,
We'll disturb her. She sighed again. O Zeus,
It's terrible! Asleep, and still sighing.
Mourning has made a warren in her spirit,
All that way below. Ponos! the heart
Is the devil of a medicine.

DOTO.   And I don't intend
To turn round.

TEGEUS.   I understand how you must feel.
Would it be—have you any objection
To my having a drink? I have a little wine here.
And, you probably see how it is: grief's in order,
And death's in order, and women—I can usually
Manage that too; but not all three together
At this hour of the morning. So you'll excuse me.
How about you? It would make me more comfortable
If you'd take a smell of it.

DOTO.   One for the road?

TEGEUS. One for the road.

DOTO.   It's the dust in my throat. The tomb
Is so dusty. Thanks, I will. There's no point in dying
Of everything, simultaneous.

TEGEUS.   It's lucky
I brought two bowls. I was expecting to keep
A drain for my relief when he comes in the morning.

DOTO   Are you on duty?

TEGEUS.   Yes.

DOTO.   It looks like it.

TEGEUS.   Well,
Here's your good health.

DOTO.   What good is that going to do me?
Here's to an easy crossing and not too much waiting
About on the bank. Do you have to tremble like that?

TEGEUS. The idea—I can't get used to it.

DOTO.   For a member
Of the forces, you're peculiarly queasy. I wish
Those owls were in Hades—oh no; let them stay where they are.
Have you never had nothing to do with corpses before?

TEGEUS. I've got six of them outside.

DOTO.   Morpheus, that's plenty.
  What are they doing there?

TEGEUS.   Hanging.

DOTO.   Hanging?

TEGEUS.   On trees.
  Five plane trees and a holly. The holly-berries
  Are just reddening. Another drink?

DOTO.   Why not?

TEGEUS. It's from Samos. Here's—

DOTO.   All right. Let's just drink it.
  —How did they get in that predicament?

TEGEUS. The sandy-haired fellow said we should collaborate
  With everybody; the little man said he wouldn't
  Collaborate with anybody; the old one
  Said that the Pleiades weren't sisters but cousins
  And anyway were manufactured in Lacedaemon.
  The fourth said that we hanged men for nothing.
  The other two said nothing. Now they hang
  About at the corner of the night, they're present
  And absent, horribly obsequious to every
  Move in the air, and yet they keep me standing
  For five hours at a stretch.

DOTO.   The wine has gone
  Down to my knees.

TEGEUS.   And up to your cheeks. You're looking
  Fresher. If only—

DOTO.   Madam? She never would.
  Shall I ask her?

TEGEUS.   No; no, don't dare, don't breathe it.
  This is privilege, to come so near
  To what is undeceiving and uncorrupt
  And undivided; this is the clear fashion
  For all souls, a ribbon to bind the unruly
  Curls of living, a faith, a hope, Zeus
  Yes, a fine thing. I am human, and this
  Is human fidelity, and we can be proud
  And unphilosophical.

DOTO.   I need to dance
  But I haven't the use of my legs.

TEGEUS.   No, no, don't dance,
  Or, at least, only inwards; don't dance; cry
  Again. We'll put a moat of tears
  Round her bastion of love, and save
  The world. It's something, it's more than something,
  It's regeneration, to see how a human cheek
  Can become as pale as a pool.

DOTO.   Do you love me, handsome?

TEGEUS. To have found life, after all, unambiguous!

DOTO. Did you say Yes?

TEGEUS.   Certainly; just now I love all men.

DOTO. So do I.

TEGEUS.   And the world is a good creature again.
  I'd begun to see it as mildew, verdigris,
  Rust, woodrot, or as though the sky had uttered
  An oval twirling blasphemy with occasional vistas
  In country districts. I was within an ace
  Of volunteering for overseas service. Despair
  Abroad can always nurse pleasant thoughts of home.
  Integrity, by god!

DOTO.   I love all the world
And the movement of the apple in your throat.
So shall you kiss me? It would be better, I should think,
To go moistly to Hades.

TEGEUS.   Her's is the way,
Luminous with sorrow.

DOTO.   Then I'll take
Another little swiggy. I love all men,
Everybody, even you, and I'll pick you
Some outrageous honeysuckle for your helmet,
If only it lived here. Pardon.

DYNAMENE.   Doto. Who is it?

DOTO. Honeysuckle, madam. Because of the bees.
Go back to sleep, madam.

DYNAMENE.   What person is it?

DOTO. Yes, I see what you mean, madam. It's a kind of
Corporal talking to his soul, on a five-hour shift,
Madam, with six bodies. He's been having his supper.

TEGEUS. I'm going. It's terrible that we should have disturbed her.

DOTO. He was delighted to see you so sad, madam.
It has stopped him going abroad.

DYNAMENE.   One with six bodies?
A messenger, a guide to where we go.
It is possible he has come to show us the way
Out of these squalid suburbs of life, a shade,
A gorgon, who has come swimming up, against
The falls of my tears (for which in truth he would need
Many limbs) to guide me to Virilius.
I shall go quietly.

TEGEUS.   I do assure you—

Such clumsiness, such a vile and unforgivable
Intrusion. I shall obliterate myself
Immediately.

DOTO.   Oblit—oh, what a pity
To oblit. Pardon. Don't let him, the nice fellow.

DYNAMENE. Sir: your other five bodies: where are they?

TEGEUS.   Madam—
Outside; I have them outside. On trees.

DYNAMENE.   Quack!

TEGEUS. What do I reply?

DYNAMENE.   Quack, charlatan!
You've never known the gods. You came to mock me.
Doto, this never was a gorgon, never.
Nor a gentleman either. He's completely spurious.
Admit it, you creature. Have you even a feather
Of the supernatural in your system? Have you?

TEGEUS. Some of my relations—

DYNAMENE.   Well?

TEGEUS.   Are dead, I think;
That is to say I have connexions—

DYNAMENE.   Connexions
With pickpockets. It's a shameless imposition.
Does the army provide you with no amusements?
If I were still of the world, and not cloistered
In a colourless landscape of winter thought
Where the approaching Spring is desired oblivion,
I should write sharply to your commanding officer.
It should be done, it should be done. If my fingers
Weren't so cold I would do it now. But they are,
Horribly cold. And why should insolence matter

When my colour of life is unreal, a blush on death,
A partial mere diaphane? I don't know
Why it should matter. Oafish, non-commissioned
Young man! The boots of your conscience will pinch for ever
If life's dignity has any self-protection.
Oh, I have to sit down. The tomb's going round.

DOTO. Oh, madam, don't give over. I can't remember
When things were so lively. He looks marvellously
Marvellously uncomfortable. Go on, madam.
Can't you, madam? Oh, madam, don't you feel up to it?
There, do you see her, you acorn-chewing infantryman?
You've made her cry, you square-bashing barbarian.

TEGEUS. O history, my private history, why
Was I led here? What stigmatism has got
Into my stars? Why wasn't it my brother?
He has a tacit misunderstanding with everybody
And washes in it. Why wasn't it my mother?
She makes a collection of other people's tears
And dries them all. Let them forget I came;
And lie in the terrible black crystal of grief
Which held them, before I broke it. Outside, Tegeus.

DOTO. Hey, I don't think so, I shouldn't say so. Come
Down again, uniform. Do you think you're going
To half kill an unprotected lady and then
Back out upwards? Do you think you can leave her like this?

TEGEUS. Yes, yes, I'll leave her. O directorate of gods,
How can I? Beauty's bit is between my teeth.
She has added another torture to me. Bottom
Of Hades' bottom.

DOTO.   Madam. Madam, the corporal
Has some wine here. It will revive you, madam.
And then you can go at him again, madam.

TEGEUS. It's the opposite of everything you've said,
I swear. I swear by Horkos and the Styx,
I swear by the nine acres of Tityos,
I swear the Hypnotic oath, by all the Titans—
By Koeos, Krios, Iapetos, Kronos, and so on—
By the three Hekatoncheires, by the insomnia
Of Tisiphone, by Jove, by jove, and the dew
On the feet of my boyhood, I am innocent
Of mocking you. Am I a Salmoneus
That, seeing such a flame of sorrow—

DYNAMENE.   You needn't
Labour to prove your secondary education.
Perhaps I jumped to a wrong conclusion, perhaps
I was hasty.

DOTO.   How easy to swear if you're properly educated.
Wasn't it pretty, madam? Pardon.

DYNAMENE.   If I misjudged you
I apologize, I apologize. Will you please leave us?
You were wrong to come here. In a place of mourning
Light itself is a trespasser; nothing can have
The right of entrance except those natural symbols
Of mortality, the jabbing, funeral, sleek-
With-omen raven, the death-watch beetle which mocks
Time: particularly, I'm afraid, the spider
Weaving his home with swift self-generated
Threads of slaughter; and, of course, the worm.
I wish it could be otherwise. Oh dear,
They aren't easy to live with.

DOTO.   Not even a *little* wine, madam?

DYNAMENE. Here, Doto?

DOTO.   Well, on the steps perhaps,
Except it's so draughty.

DYNAMENE.   Doto! Here?

DOTO.   No, madam;
  I quite see.

DYNAMENE. I might be wise to strengthen myself
  In order to fast again; it would make me abler
  For grief. I will breathe a little of it, Doto.

DOTO. Thank god. Where's the bottle?

DYNAMENE.   What an exquisite bowl.

TEGEUS. Now that it's peacetime we have pottery classes.

DYNAMENE. You made it yourself?

TEGEUS.   Yes. Do you see the design?
  The corded god, tied also by the rays
  Of the sun, and the astonished ship erupting
  Into vines and vine-leaves, inverted pyramids
  Of grapes, the uplifted hands of the men (the raiders),
  And here the headlong sea, itself almost
  Venturing into leaves and tendrils, and Proteus
  With his beard braiding the wind, and this
  Held by other hands is a drowned sailor—

DYNAMENE. Always, always.

DOTO.   Hold the bowl steady, madam.
  Pardon.

DYNAMENE. Doto, have you been drinking?

DOTO.   Here, madam?
  I coaxed some a little way towards my mouth, madam,
  But I scarcely swallowed except because I had to. The hiccup
  Is from no breakfast, madam, and not meant to be funny.

DYNAMENE. You may drink this too. Oh, how the inveterate body,
  Even when cut from the heart, insists on leaf,
  Puts out, with a separate meaningless will,

Fronds to intercept the thankless sun.
How it does, oh, how it does. And how it confuses
The nature of the mind.

TEGEUS.   Yes, yes, the confusion;
That's something I understand better than anything.

DYNAMENE. When the thoughts would die, the instincts will set
    sail
For life. And when the thoughts are alert for life
The instincts will rage to be destroyed on the rocks.
To Virilius it was not so; his brain was an ironing-board
For all crumpled indecision: and I follow him,
The hawser of my world. You don't belong here,
You see; you don't belong here at all.

TEGEUS.   If only
I did. If only you knew the effort it costs me
To mount those steps again into an untrustworthy,
Unpredictable, unenlightened night,
And turn my back on—on a state of affairs,
I can only call it a vision, a hope, a promise,
A— By that I mean loyalty, enduring passion,
Unrecking bravery and beauty all in one.

DOTO. He means you, or you and me; or me, madam.

TEGEUS. It only remains for me to thank you, and to say
That whatever awaits me and for however long
I may be played by this poor musician, existence,
Your person and sacrifice will leave their trace
As clear upon me as the shape of the hills
Around my birthplace. Now I must leave you to your husband.

DOTO. Oh! You, madam.

DYNAMENE.   I'll tell you what I will do.
I will drink with you to the memory of my husband,

Because I have been curt, because you are kind,
And because I'm extremely thirsty. And then we will say
Good-bye and part to go to our opposite corruptions,
The world and the grave.

TEGEUS.   The climax to the vision.

DYNAMENE [*drinking*]. My husband, and all he stood for.

TEGEUS.   Stands for.

DYNAMENE.   Stands for.

TEGEUS. Your husband.

DOTO.   The master.

DYNAMENE.   How good it is,
How it sings to the throat, purling with summer.

TEGEUS. It has a twin nature, winter and warmth in one,
Moon and meadow. Do you agree?

DYNAMENE.   Perfectly;
A cold bell sounding in a golden month.

TEGEUS. Crystal in harvest.

DYNAMENE.   Perhaps a nightingale
Sobbing among the pears.

TEGEUS.   In an old autumnal midnight.

DOTO. Grapes.—Pardon. There's some more here.

TEGEUS.   Plenty.
I drink to the memory of your husband.

DYNAMENE.   My husband.

DOTO.   The master.

DYNAMENE. He was careless in his choice of wines.

TEGEUS.   And yet
Rendering to living its rightful poise is not
Unimportant.

DYNAMENE.   A mystery's in the world
Where a little liquid, with flavour, quality, and fume
Can be as no other, can hint and flute our senses
As though a music played in harvest hollows
And a movement was in the swathes of our memory.
Why should scent, why should flavour come
With such wings upon us? Parsley, for instance.

TEGEUS. Seaweed.

DYNAMENE.   Lime trees.

DOTO.   Horses.

TEGEUS.   Fruit in the fire.

DYNAMENE. Do I know your name?

TEGEUS.   Tegeus.

DYNAMENE.   That's very thin for you,
It hardly covers your bones. Something quite different,
Altogether other. I shall think of it presently.

TEGEUS. Darker vowels, perhaps.

DYNAMENE.   Yes, certainly darker vowels.
And your consonants should have a slight angle.
And a certain temperature. Do you know what I mean?
It will come to me.

TEGEUS.   Now *your* name—

DYNAMENE.   It is nothing
To any purpose. I'll be to you the She
In the tomb. You have the air of a natural-historian
As though you were accustomed to handling birds' eggs,
Or tadpoles, or putting labels on moths. You see?
The genius of dumb things, that they are nameless.
Have I found the seat of the weevil in human brains?
Our names. They make us broody; we sit and sit

To hatch them into reputation and dignity.
And then they set upon us and become despair,
Guilt and remorse. We go where they lead. We dance
Attendance on something wished upon us by the wife
Of our mother's physician. But insects meet and part
And put the woods about them, fill the dusk
And freckle the light and go and come without
A name among them, without the wish of a name
And very pleasant too. Did I interrupt you?

TEGEUS. I forget. We'll have no names then.

DYNAMENE.   I should like
You to have a name, I don't know why; a small one
To fill out the conversation.

TEGEUS.   I should like
You to have a name too, if only for something
To remember. Have you still some wine in your bowl?

DYNAMENE. Not altogether.

TEGEUS.   We haven't come to the end
By several inches. Did I splash you?

DYNAMENE.   It doesn't matter.
Well, here's to my husband's name.

TEGEUS.   Your husband's name.

DOTO. The master.

DYNAMENE.   It was kind of you to come.

TEGEUS. It was more than coming. I followed my future here,
As we all do if we're sufficiently inattentive
And don't vex ourselves with questions; or do I mean
Attentive? If so, attentive to what? Do I sound
Incoherent?

B

DYNAMENE. You're wrong. There isn't a future here,
Not here, not for you.

TEGEUS.   Your name's Dynamene.

DYNAMENE. Who—Have I been utterly irreverent? Are you—
Who made you say that? Forgive me the question,
But are you dark or light? I mean which shade
Of the supernatural? Or if neither, what prompted you?

TEGEUS. Dynamene——

DYNAMENE.   No, but I'm sure you're the friend of nature,
It must be so, I think I see little Phoebuses
Rising and setting in your eyes.

DOTO.   They're not little Phoebuses,
They're hoodwinks, madam. Your name is on your brooch.
No little Phoebuses to-night.

DYNAMENE.   That's twice
You've played me a trick. Oh, I know practical jokes
Are common on Olympus, but haven't we at all
Developed since the gods were born? Are gods
And men both to remain immortal adolescents?
How tiresome it all is.

TEGEUS.   It was you, each time,
Who said I was supernatural. When did I say so?
You're making me into whatever you imagine
And then you blame me because I can't live up to it.

DYNAMENE. I shall call you Chromis. It has a breadlike sound.
I think of you as a crisp loaf.

TEGEUS.   And now
You'll insult me because I'm not sliceable.

DYNAMENE. I think drinking is harmful to our tempers.

TEGEUS. If I seem to be frowning, that is only because
    I'm looking directly into your light: I must look
    Angrily, or shut my eyes.

DYNAMENE.   Shut them.—Oh,
    You have eyelashes! A new perspective of you.
    Is that how you look when you sleep?

TEGEUS.   My jaw drops down.

DYNAMENE. Show me how.

TEGEUS.   Like this.

DYNAMENE.   It makes an irresistible
    Moron of you. Will you waken now?
    It's morning; I see a thin dust of daylight
    Blowing on to the steps.

TEGEUS.   Already? Dynamene,
    You're tricked again. This time by the moon.

DYNAMENE.   Oh well,
    Moon's daylight, then. Doto is asleep.

TEGEUS.   Doto
    Is asleep . . .

DYNAMENE.   Chromis, what made you walk about
    In the night? What, I wonder, made you not stay
    Sleeping wherever you slept? Was it the friction
    Of the world on your mind? Those two are difficult
    To make agree. Chromis—now try to learn
    To answer your name. I won't say Tegeus.

TEGEUS.   And I
    Won't say Dynamene.

DYNAMENE.   Not?

TEGEUS.   It makes you real.
    Forgive me, a terrible thing has happened. Shall I

Say it and perhaps destroy myself for you?
Forgive me first, or, more than that, forgive
Nature who winds her furtive stream all through
Our reason. Do you forgive me?

DYNAMENE.   I'll forgive
Anything, if it's the only way I can know
What you have to tell me.

TEGEUS.   I felt us to be alone;
Here in a grave, separate from any life,
I and the only one of beauty, the only
Persuasive key to all my senses,
In spite of my having lain day after day
And pored upon the sepals, corolla, stamen, and bracts
Of the yellow bog-iris. Then my body ventured
A step towards interrupting your perfection of purpose
And my own renewed faith in human nature.
Would you have believed that possible?

DYNAMENE.   I have never
Been greatly moved by the yellow bog-iris. Alas,
It's as I said. This place is for none but the spider,
Raven and worms, not for a living man.

TEGEUS. It has been a place of blessing to me. It will always
Play in me, a fountain of confidence
When the world is arid. But I know it is true
I have to leave it, and though it withers my soul
I must let you make your journey.

DYNAMENE.   No.

TEGEUS.   Not true?

DYNAMENE. We can talk of something quite different.

TEGEUS.   Yes, we can!
Oh yes, we will! Is it your opinion

That no one believes who hasn't learned to doubt?
Or, another thing, if we persuade ourselves
To one particular Persuasion, become Sophist,
Stoic, Platonist, anything whatever,
Would you say that there must be areas of soul
Lying unproductive therefore, or dishonoured
Or blind?

DYNAMENE.   No, I don't know.

TEGEUS.   No. It's impossible
To tell. Dynamene, if only I had
Two cakes of pearl-barley and hydromel
I could see you to Hades, leave you with your husband
And come back to the world.

DYNAMENE.   Ambition, I suppose,
Is an appetite particular to man.
What is your definition?

TEGEUS.   The desire to find
A reason for living.

DYNAMENE.   But then, suppose it leads,
As often, one way or another, it does, to death.

TEGEUS. Then that may be life's reason. Oh, but how
Could I bear to return, Dynamene? The earth's
Daylight would be my grave if I had left you
In that unearthly night.

DYNAMENE.   O Chromis——

TEGEUS.   Tell me,
What is your opinion of Progress? Does it, for example,
Exist? Is there ever progression without retrogression?
Therefore is it not true that mankind
Can more justly be said increasingly to Gress?

As the material improves, the craftsmanship deteriorates
And honour and virtue remain the same. I love you,
Dynamene.

DYNAMENE. Would you consider we go round and round?

TEGEUS. We concertina, I think; taking each time
A larger breath, so that the farther we go out
The farther we have to go in.

DYNAMENE.   There'll come a time
When it will be unbearable to continue.

TEGEUS. Unbearable.

DYNAMENE.   Perhaps we had better have something
To eat. The wine has made your eyes so quick
I am breathless beside them. It *is*
Your eyes, I think; or your intelligence
Holding my intelligence up above you
Between its hands. Or the cut of your uniform.

TEGEUS. Here's a new roll with honey. In the gods' names
Let's sober ourselves.

DYNAMENE.   As soon as possible.

TEGEUS.   Have you
Any notion of algebra?

DYNAMENE.   We'll discuss you, Chromis.
We will discuss you, till you're nothing but words.

TEGEUS. I? There is nothing, of course, I would rather discuss,
Except—if it would be no intrusion—you, Dynamene.

DYNAMENE. No, you couldn't want to. But your birthplace,
    Chromis,
With the hills that placed themselves in you for ever
As you say, where was it?

TEGEUS.   My father's farm at Pyxa.

DYNAMENE. There? Could it be there?

TEGEUS.   I was born in the hills
Between showers, a quarter of an hour before milking time.
Do you know Pyxa? It stretches to the crossing of two
Troublesome roads, and buries its back in beechwood,
From which come the white owls of our nights
And the mulling and cradling of doves in the day.
I attribute my character to those shadows
And heavy roots; and my interest in music
To the sudden melodious escape of the young river
Where it breaks from nosing through the cresses and kingcups.
That's honestly so.

DYNAMENE.   You used to climb about
Among the windfallen tower of Phrasidemus
Looking for bees' nests.

TEGEUS.   What? When have I
Said so?

DYNAMENE.   Why, all the children did.

TEGEUS. Yes: but, in the name of light, how do you *know* that?

DYNAMENE. I played there once, on holiday.

TEGEUS.   O Klotho,
Lachesis and Atropos!

DYNAMENE.   It's the strangest chance:
I may have seen, for a moment, your boyhood.

TEGEUS.   I may
Have seen something like an early flower
Something like a girl. If I only could remember how I must
Have seen you. Were you after the short white violets?
Maybe I blundered past you, taking your look,
And scarcely acknowledged how a star

Ran through me, to live in the brooks of my blood for ever.
Or I saw you playing at hiding in the cave
Where the ferns are and the water drips.

DYNAMENE. I was quite plain and fat and I was usually
Hitting someone. I wish I could remember you.
I'm envious of the days and children who saw you
Then. It is curiously a little painful
Not to share your past.

TEGEUS.   How did it come
Our stars could mingle for an afternoon
So long ago, and then forget us or tease us
Or helplessly look on the dark high seas
Of our separation, while time drank
The golden hours? What hesitant fate is that?

DYNAMENE. Time? Time? Why—how old are we?

TEGEUS.   Young,
Thank both our mothers, but still we're older than to-night
And so older than we should be. Wasn't I born
In love with what, only now, I have grown to meet?
I'll tell you something else. I was born entirely
For this reason. I was born to fill a gap
In the world's experience, which had never known
Chromis loving Dynamene.

DYNAMENE.   You are so
Excited, poor Chromis. What is it? Here you sit
With a woman who has wept away all claims
To appearance, unbecoming in her oldest clothes,
With not a trace of liveliness, a drab
Of melancholy, entirely shadow without
A smear of sun. Forgive me if I tell you
That you fall easily into superlatives.

TEGEUS. Very well. I'll say nothing, then. I'll fume
  With feeling.

DYNAMENE.   Now you go to the extreme. Certainly
  You must speak. You may have more to say. Besides
  You might let your silence run away with you
  And not say something that you should. And how
  Should I answer you then? Chromis, you boy,
  I can't look away from you. You use
  The lamplight and the moon so skilfully,
  So arrestingly, in and around your furrows.
  A humorous ploughman goes whistling to a team
  Of sad sorrow, to and fro in your brow
  And over your arable cheek. Laugh for me. Have you
  Cried for women, ever?

TEGEUS.   In looking about for you.
  But I have recognized them for what they were.

DYNAMENE. What were they?

TEGEUS.   Never you: never, although
  They could walk with bright distinction into all men's
  Longest memories, never you, by a hint
  Or a faint quality, or at least not more
  Than reflectively, stars lost and uncertain
  In the sea, compared with the shining salt, the shiners,
  The galaxies, the clusters, the bright grain whirling
  Over the black threshing-floor of space.
  Will you make some effort to believe that?

DYNAMENE.   No, no effort.
  It lifts me and carries me. It may be wild
  But it comes to me with a charm, like trust indeed,
  And eats out of my heart, dear Chromis,
  Absurd, disconcerting Chromis. You make me

Feel I wish I could look my best for you.
I wish, at least, that I could believe myself
To be showing some beauty for you, to put in the scales
Between us. But they dip to you, they sink
With masculine victory.

TEGEUS.   Eros, no! No!
If this is less than your best, then never, in my presence,
Be more than your less: never! If you should bring
More to your mouth or to your eyes, a moisture
Or a flake of light, anything, anything fatally
More, perfection would fetch her unsparing rod
Out of pickle to flay me, and what would have been love
Will be the end of me. O Dynamene,
Let me unload something of my lips' longing
On to yours receiving. Oh, when I cross
Like this the hurt of the little space between us
I come a journey from the wrenching ice
To walk in the sun. That is the feeling.

DYNAMENE.   Chromis,
Where am I going? No, don't answer. It's death
I desire, not you.

TEGEUS.   Where is the difference? Call me
Death instead of Chromis. I'll answer to anything.
It's desire all the same, of death in me, or me
In death, but Chromis either way. Is it so?
Do you not love me, Dynamene?

DYNAMENE.   How could it happen?
I'm going to my husband. I'm too far on the way
To admit myself to life again. Love's in Hades.

TEGEUS. Also here. And here are we, not there
In Hades. Is your husband expecting you?

DYNAMENE. Surely, surely?

TEGEUS.   Not necessarily. I,
  If I had been your husband, would never dream
  Of expecting you. I should remember your body
  Descending stairs in the floating light, but not
  Descending in Hades. I should say 'I have left
  My wealth warm on the earth, and, hell, earth needs it.'
  'Was all I taught her of love,' I should say, 'so poor
  That she will leave her flesh and become shadow?'
  'Wasn't our love for each other' (I should continue)
  'Infused with life, and life infused with our love?
  Very well; repeat me in love, repeat me in life,
  And let me sing in your blood for ever.'

DYNAMENE. Stop, stop, I shall be dragged apart!
  Why should the fates do everything to keep me
  From dying honourably? They must have got
  Tired of honour in Elysium. Chromis, it's terrible
  To be susceptible to two conflicting norths.
  I have the constitution of a whirlpool.
  Am I actually twirling, or is it just sensation?

TEGEUS. You're still; still as the darkness.

DYNAMENE.   What appears
  Is so unlike what is. And what is madness
  To those who only observe, is often wisdom
  To those to whom it happens.

TEGEUS.   Are we compelled
  To go into all this?

DYNAMENE.   Why, how could I return
  To my friends? Am I to be an entertainment?

TEGEUS. That's for to-morrow. To-night I need to kiss you,
  Dynamene. Let's see what the whirlpool does

Between my arms; let it whirl on my breast. O love,
Come in.

DYNAMENE. I am there before I reach you; my body
Only follows to join my longing which
Is holding you already.—Now I am
All one again.

TEGEUS.   I feel as the gods feel:
This is their sensation of life, not a man's:
Their suspension of immortality, to enrich
Themselves with time. O life, O death, O body,
O spirit, O Dynamene.

DYNAMENE.   O all
In myself; it so covets all in you,
My care, my Chromis. Then I shall be
Creation.

TEGEUS.   You have the skies already;
Out of them you are buffeting me with your gales
Of beauty. Can we be made of dust, as they tell us?
What! dust with dust releasing such a light
And such an apparition of the world
Within one body? A thread of your hair has stung me.
Why do you push me away?

DYNAMENE.   There's so much metal
About you. Do I have to be imprisoned
In an armoury?

TEGEUS.   Give your hand to the buckles and then
To me.

DYNAMENE. Don't help; I'll do them all myself.

TEGEUS. O time and patience! I want you back again.

DYNAMENE. We have a lifetime. O Chromis, think, think
Of that. And even unfastening a buckle

Is loving. And not easy. Very well,
You can help me. Chromis, what zone of miracle
Did you step into to direct you in the dark
To where I waited, not knowing I waited?

TEGEUS.   I saw
The lamplight. That was only the appearance
Of some great gesture in the bed of fortune.
I saw the lamplight.

DYNAMENE.   But here? So far from life?
What brought you near enough to see lamplight?

TEGEUS.   Zeus,
That reminds me.

DYNAMENE.   What is it, Chromis?

TEGEUS.   I'm on duty.

DYNAMENE. Is it warm enough to do without your greaves?

TEGEUS. Darling loom of magic, I must go back
To take a look at those boys. The whole business
Of guard had gone out of my mind.

DYNAMENE.   What boys, my heart?

TEGEUS. My six bodies.

DYNAMENE.   Chromis, not that joke
Again.

TEGEUS. No joke, sweet. To-day our city
Held a sextuple hanging. I'm minding the bodies
Until five o'clock. Already I've been away
For half an hour.

DYNAMENE.   What can they do, poor bodies,
In half an hour, or half a century?
You don't really mean to go?

TEGEUS.   Only to make
  My conscience easy. Then, Dynamene,
  No cloud can rise on love, no hovering thought
  Fidget, and the night will be only to *us*.

DYNAMENE. But if every half-hour——

TEGEUS.   Hush, smile of my soul,
  My sprig, my sovereign: this is to hold your eyes,
  I sign my lips on them both: this is to keep
  Your forehead—do you feel the claim of my kiss
  Falling into your thought? And now your throat
  Is a white branch and my lips two singing birds—
  They are coming to rest. Throat, remember me
  Until I come back in five minutes. Over all
  Here is my parole: I give it to your mouth
  To give me again before it's dry. I promise:
  Before it's dry, or not long after.

DYNAMENE.   Run,
  Run all the way. You needn't be afraid of stumbling.
  There's plenty of moon. The fields are blue. Oh, wait,
  Wait! My darling. No, not now: it will keep
  Until I see you; I'll have it here at my lips.
  Hurry.

TEGEUS. So long, my haven.

DYNAMENE.   Hurry, hurry!

                                        [*Exit* TEGEUS.

DOTO. Yes, madam, hurry; of course. Are we there
  Already? How nice. Death doesn't take
  Any doing at all. We were gulped into Hades
  As easy as an oyster.

DYNAMENE.   Doto!

DOTO.   Hurry, hurry,
Yes, madam.—But they've taken out all my bones.
I haven't a bone left. I'm a Shadow: wonderfully shady
In the legs. We shall have to sit out eternity, madam,
If they've done the same to you.

DYNAMENE.   You'd better wake up.
If you can't go to sleep again, you'd better wake up.
Oh dear.—We're still alive, Doto, do you hear me?

DOTO. You must speak for yourself, madam. I'm quite dead.
I'll tell you how I know. I feel
Invisible. I'm a wraith, madam; I'm only
Waiting to be wafted.

DYNAMENE.   If only you *would* be.
Do you see where you are? Look. Do you see?

DOTO. Yes. You're right, madam. We're still alive.
Isn't it enough to make you swear?
Here we are, dying to be dead,
And where does it get us?

DYNAMENE.   Perhaps you should try to die
In some other place. Yes! Perhaps the air here
Suits you too well. You were sleeping very heavily.

DOTO. And all the time you alone and dying.
I shouldn't have. Has the corporal been long gone,
Madam?

DYNAMENE.   He came and went, came and went,
You know the way.

DOTO.   Very well I do. And went
He should have, come he should never. Oh dear, he must
Have disturbed you, madam.

DYNAMENE.   He could be said
To've disturbed me. Listen; I have something to say to you.

DOTO. I expect so, madam. Maybe I *could* have kept him out
But men are in before I wish they wasn't.
I think quickly enough, but I get behindhand
With what I ought to be saying. It's a kind of stammer
In my way of life, madam.

DYNAMENE.   I have been unkind,
I have sinfully wronged you, Doto.

DOTO.   Never, madam.

DYNAMENE. Oh yes. I was letting you die with me, Doto, without
Any fair reason. I was drowning you
In grief that wasn't yours. That was wrong, Doto.

DOTO. But I haven't got anything against dying, madam.
I may *like* the situation, as far as I like
Any situation, madam. Now if you'd said mangling,
A lot of mangling, I might have thought twice about staying.
We all have our dislikes, madam.

DYNAMENE.   I'm asking you
To leave me, Doto, at once, as quickly as possible,
Now, before—now, Doto, and let me forget
My bad mind which confidently expected you
To companion me to Hades. Now good-bye,
Good-bye.

DOTO.   No, it's not good-bye at all.
I shouldn't know another night of sleep, wondering
How you got on, or what I was missing, come to that.
I should be anxious about you, too. When you belong
To an upper class, the netherworld might come strange.
Now I was born nether, madam, though not
As nether as some. No, it's not good-bye, madam.

DYNAMENE. Oh Doto, go; you must, you must! And if I seem
Without gratitude, forgive me. It isn't so,

It is far, far from so. But I can only
Regain my peace of mind if I know you're gone.

DOTO. Besides, look at the time, madam. Where should I go
At three in the morning? Even if I was to think
Of going; and think of it I never shall.

DYNAMENE. Think of the unmatchable world, Doto.

DOTO.   I do
Think of it, madam. And when I think of it, what
Have I thought? Well, it depends, madam.

DYNAMENE.   I insist,
Obey me! At once! Doto!

DOTO.   Here I sit.

DYNAMENE. What shall I do with you?

DOTO.   Ignore me, madam.
I know my place. I shall die quite unobtrusive.
Oh look, the corporal's forgotten to take his equipment.

DYNAMENE. Could he be so careless?

DOTO.   I shouldn't hardly have thought so.
Poor fellow. They'll go and deduct it off his credits.
I suppose, madam, I suppose he couldn't be thinking
Of coming back?

DYNAMENE.   He'll think of these. He will notice
He isn't wearing them. He'll come; he is sure to come.

DOTO. Oh.

DYNAMENE. I know he will.

DOTO.   Oh, oh.
Is that all for to-night, madam? May I go now, madam?

DYNAMENE. Doto! Will you?

DOTO.   Just you try to stop me, madam.
  Sometimes going is a kind of instinct with me.
  I'll leave death to some other occasion.

DYNAMENE.   Do,
  Doto. Any other time. Now you must hurry.
  I won't delay you from life another moment.
  Oh, Doto, good-bye.

DOTO.   Good-bye. Life is unusual,
  Isn't it, madam? Remember me to Cerberus.
                   [*Re-enter* TEGEUS. DOTO *passes him on the steps.*

DOTO [*as she goes*]. You left something behind. Ye gods, what a
  moon!

DYNAMENE. Chromis, it's true; my lips are hardly dry.
  Time runs again; the void is space again;
  Space has life again; Dynamene has Chromis.

TEGEUS. It's over.

DYNAMENE.   Chromis, you're sick. As white as wool.
  Come, you covered the distance too quickly.
  Rest in my arms; get your breath again.

TEGEUS. I've breathed one night too many. Why did I see you,
  Why in the name of life did I see you?

DYNAMENE.   Why?
  Weren't we gifted with each other? O heart,
  What do you mean?

TEGEUS.   I mean that joy is nothing
  But the parent of doom. Why should I have found
  Your constancy such balm to the world and yet
  Find, by the same vision, its destruction
  A necessity? We're set upon by love
  To make us incompetent to steer ourselves,

To make us docile to fate. I should have known:
Indulgences, not fulfilment, is what the world
Permits us.

DYNAMENE. Chromis, is this intelligible?
Help me to follow you. What did you meet in the fields
To bring about all this talk? Do you still love me?

TEGEUS. What good will it do us? I've lost a body.

DYNAMENE.   A body?
One of the six? Well, it isn't with them you propose
To love me; and you couldn't keep it for ever.
Are we going to allow a body that isn't there
To come between us?

TEGEUS.   But I'm responsible for it.
I have to account for it in the morning. Surely
You see, Dynamene, the horror we're faced with?
The relatives have had time to cut him down
And take him away for burial. It means
A court martial. No doubt about the sentence.
I shall take the place of the missing man.
To be hanged, Dynamene! Hanged, Dynamene!

DYNAMENE. No; it's monstrous! Your life is yours, Chromis.

TEGEUS. Anything but. That's why I have to take it.
At the best we live our lives on loan,
At the worst in chains. And I was never born
To have life. Then for what? To be had by it,
And so are we all. But I'll make it what it is,
By making it nothing.

DYNAMENE.   Chromis, you're frightening me.
What are you meaning to do?

TEGEUS.   I have to die,
Dance of my heart, I have to die, to die,

To part us, to go to my sword and let it part us.
I'll have my free will even if I'm compelled to it.
I'll kill myself.

DYNAMENE.   Oh, no! No, Chromis!
It's all unreasonable—no such horror
Can come of a pure accident. Have you hanged?
How can they hang you for simply not being somewhere?
How can they hang you for losing a dead man?
They must have wanted to lose him, or they wouldn't
Have hanged him. No, you're scaring yourself for nothing
And making me frantic.

TEGEUS.   It's section six, paragraph
Three in the Regulations. That's my doom.
I've read it for myself. And, by my doom,
Since I have to die, let me die here, in love,
Promoted by your kiss to tower, in dying,
High above my birth. For god's sake let me die
On a wave of life, Dynamene, with an action
I can take some pride in. How could I settle to death
Knowing that you last saw me stripped and strangled
On a holly tree? Demoted first and then hanged!

DYNAMENE. Am I supposed to love the corporal
Or you? It's you I love, from head to foot
And out to the ends of your spirit. What shall I do
If you die? How could I follow you? I should find you
Discussing me with my husband, comparing your feelings,
Exchanging reactions. Where should I put myself?
Or am I to live on alone, or find in life
Another source of love, in memory
Of Virilius and of you?

TEGEUS.   Dynamene,
Not that! Since everything in the lives of men

Is brief to indifference, let our love at least
Echo and perpetuate itself uniquely
As long as time allows you. Though you go
To the limit of age, it won't be far to contain me.

DYNAMENE. It will seem like eternity ground into days and days.

TEGEUS. Can I be certain of you, for ever?

DYNAMENE.   But, Chromis,
Surely you said——

TEGEUS.   Surely we have sensed
Our passion to be greater than mortal? Must I
Die believing it is dying with me?

DYNAMENE.   Chromis,
You must never die, never! It would be
An offence against truth.

TEGEUS.   I cannot live to be hanged.
It would be an offence against life. Give me my sword,
Dynamene. O Hades, when you look pale
You take the heart out of me. I could die
Without a sword by seeing you suffer. Quickly!
Give me my heart back again with your lips
And I'll live the rest of my ambitions
In a last kiss.

DYNAMENE.   Oh, no, no, no!
Give my blessing to your desertion of me?
Never, Chromis, never. Kiss you and then
Let you go? Love you, for death to have you?
Am I to be made the fool of courts martial?
Who are they who think they can discipline souls
Right off the earth? What discipline is that?
Chromis, love is the only discipline

And we're the disciples of love. I hold you to that:
Hold you, hold you.

TEGEUS.   We have no chance. It's determined
In section six, paragraph three, of the Regulations.
That has more power than love. It can snuff the great
Candles of creation. It makes me able
To do the impossible, to leave you, to go from the light
That keeps you.

DYNAMENE.   No!

TEGEUS.   O dark, it does. Good-bye,
My memory of earth, my dear most dear
Beyond every expectation. I was wrong
To want you to keep our vows existent
In the vacuum that's coming. It would make you
A heaviness to the world, when you should be,
As you are, a form of light. Dynamene, turn
Your head away. I'm going to let my sword
Solve all the riddles.

DYNAMENE.   Chromis, I have it! I know!
Virilius will help you.

TEGEUS.   Virilius?

DYNAMENE. My husband. He can be the other body.

TEGEUS. Your husband can?

DYNAMENE.   He has no further use
For what he left of himself to lie with us here.
Is there any reason why he shouldn't hang
On your holly tree? Better, far better, he,
Than you who are still alive, and surely better
Than *idling* into corruption?

TEGEUS.   Hang your husband?
Dynamene, it's terrible, horrible.

DYNAMENE. How little you can understand. I loved
His life not his death. And now we can give his death
The power of life. Not horrible: wonderful!
Isn't it so? That I should be able to feel
He moves again in the world, accomplishing
Our welfare? It's more than my grief could do.

TEGEUS. What can I say?

DYNAMENE.   That you love me; as I love him
And you. Let's celebrate your safety then.
Where's the bottle? There's some wine unfinished in this bowl.
I'll share it with you. Now forget the fear
We were in; look at me, Chromis. Come away
From the pit you nearly dropped us in. My darling,
I give you Virilius.

TEGEUS.   Virilius.
And all that follows.

DOTO [*on the steps, with the bottle*]. The master. Both the masters.

CURTAIN

THOR, WITH ANGELS

A Play

*First performed at the Canterbury Festival
in June 1948*

CHARACTERS

CYMEN
CLODESUIDA, *His Wife*
MARTINA, *His Daughter*
QUICHELM, *His Elder Son*
CHELDRIC, *His Younger Son*
TADFRID ⎞
          ⎬ *His Brothers-in-Law*
OSMER   ⎠
COLGRIN, *His Steward*
ANNA, *Colgrin's Wife*
HOEL, *A British Prisoner*
MERLIN
A MESSENGER

SCENE: *A Jutish Farmstead*, A.D. 596

A Jutish farmstead, both within and without. To the left a group of trees; to the right a shed, in which COLGRIN, *an elderly man, is asleep among the straw. Enter* QUICHELM. *He hammers at the farm door.*

QUICHELM. Hyo, there! Who's awake? Where's
The welcome of women for warfarers?
Where's my Wodenfearing mother?
Hey! hey! Spare some sleep for us:
Leave us half a snore and a stale dream.
Here's your battery of males come home!
Our bones are aching; we're as wet
As bogworms. Who's alive in there?

COLGRIN. There's an infernal clatter. What's the matter?
Foof! Straw in the nostrils. That's bad.
Who's blaspheming in the thick of the mist?
I've got you on my weapon's point.
(Where the Valhalla is it?)

QUICHELM.   Colgrin,
You scrawny old scurfscratcher, is that you?

COLGRIN. Frog-man, fen-fiend, werewolf, oul, elf,
Or whatever unnatural thing you are
Croaking in the voice of Master Quichelm
Who I happen to know is away waging war,
Stand away from the swiping of my sword.
(Where in thunder did I put it?)

QUICHELM. Runt of an old sow's litter, you slop-headed
Pot-scourer, come here, you buckle-backed
Gutsack, come out of there!

COLGRIN.   That's
The young master. There's not a devil
In the length of the land could pick such a posy of words

57

And not swoon smelling it. Here I come,
Here I come. Welcome home and so forth.

QUICHELM. Woden welt you for a sheeptick, where's my mother?

COLGRIN. That's a nice question. I must ponder.
Maybe asleep in her cot. Or not.

QUICHELM. I'll carve your dropsical trunk into a tassel.
Where's my sister? You were left to guard them,
Not to roll your pig-sweat in a snoring stupor.
Tell me where they are before I unbutton your throat.

MARTINA [*entering*]. We're here, Quichelm. I knew you'd come
  to-day.
The cows this morning were all facing north.
Are you whole and hale?

QUICHELM.   Look me over. Ten
Fingers. You can take the toes for granted.
Where's my mother?

MARTINA.   We went to early rite.
I wanted to stay and keep a watch out for you
But she made me go; you know what she is.

COLGRIN. That's what I said. Gone to early rite.
And my wife with her; a devout woman, but dismal
In some respects. They'll be back just now.
The sun's arisen.

QUICHELM.   You get stuck
Into some work, you whitebellied weasel.
By dugs, I think I'll strike you anyway.

COLGRIN. Wasn't I there as bright and bristling
As Barney the boarhound, just as soon as I heard
Your honour's foot creak over the bridge?

MARTINA. Beat him to-morrow. Let's be affable.
Is father all right? And Cheldric?

QUICHELM.   Cheldric's all right.

MARTINA. Why not father? Stop picking at your teeth.
Something is wrong. Was father killed?
I knew it. The house was crowned with crows this morning.

QUICHELM. Shut up. None of us is killed.
Are you still here?

COLGRIN [*going in*]. No, sir, no. It's what
You remember of me. There's trouble coming. I see that.

Enter CLODESUIDA *and* ANNA.

CLODESUIDA. Quichelm, you're back! Oh, fortunate day.

ANNA. Welcome home.

QUICHELM.   Yes, the battle's finished.

CLODESUIDA [*to* ANNA]. Rouse the fire up; and find them food.
[*Exit* ANNA.

MARTINA. Don't expect pleasure.

CLODESUIDA.   Something is wrong. Is your father
With you, and well?

QUICHELM.   He's much as when you saw him.

CLODESUIDA. Much? What's that, much? Has he been hurt?

QUICHELM. No weapon has touched him.

CLODESUIDA.   Then he's ill?
Why do you talk to me in a kind of cloud?
What has happened?

QUICHELM.   Mother, we breathe cloud.
It's the chief product of this island.

C

CLODESUIDA.   Don't provoke me!
  Where is your father?

QUICHELM.   Coming up the hill.

MARTINA. Dimly, yes; I can just see the shapes of them.

CLODESUIDA. And Cheldric, too? And your uncles?
  Yes,
  They all come. The mist is confusing. I could imagine
  There are five of them.

QUICHELM.   So there are. My father
  Brings a prisoner.

CLODESUIDA.   A prisoner? Are we
  To have an intolerable Saxon here?

QUICHELM. An even greater strain on your toleration:
  A Briton. A British slave who fought for the Saxons.

CLODESUIDA. But why? Why bring a benighted Briton here?
  I thought those heathen had been tidied away, once
  And for all. And the country's healthier for it.
  Your father's demented.

QUICHELM.   You would have said so
  If you had seen him as we saw him in the battle.
  Like a madman, he saved this Briton when we'd have killed him:
  Burst in among us, blaspheming against Woden,
  Broke his sword in the air—he swore it broke
  Against a staggering light—and stood roaring,
  Swaying in a sweat of wax, bestraddled
  Over the fallen Briton. And then, as though
  The beast which had bragged in his brain had leapt away,
  Became himself again,
  Only in a fury with the light which broke his sword.

CLODESUIDA. How could the sword have broken?

You make me afraid
To see him. Are you sure that he blasphemed?
That's the worst of all. It's hard enough
To live well-thought-of by the gods.

MARTINA.   We haven't
Enough cattle to placate them more than twice a year.
He knows we have to be careful.

QUICHELM. They're here. And you haven't heard the worst.

CLODESUIDA. The worst? What worse can there be?
Quichelm,
What else? . . .

QUICHELM. Don't let him know that I've been talking.
He'd lay me flat.

CLODESUIDA. He'll notice how I tremble.

> [*Enter to the house* CYMEN, *his brothers-in-law* TADFRID
> *and* OSMER, *and his younger son* CHELDRIC. CLODE-
> SUIDA *and* MARTINA *stand staring at him.*

CYMEN. Well? Have I come home? Or is this a place
Of graven images? What's the silence for?
I've laid down arms, so that arms
Could take me up, a natural expectation.
Where's my wife?

CLODESUIDA. You can see me. Here I am.

CYMEN. Where's my wife? Where's the head on my breast?
Better. Where's my daughter? Where's the white
Hand hanging on my shoulder? Better, better.
I'll have a cup of mead.
Where's my mead? Where the devil's my mead?
Have I got to wring the water out of my shirt
To get a drink?

COLGRIN [*appearing*]. Here's your mead, my lord:
  And the bees were proud to make themselves drunk
  To make you drunk, and welcome home, my lord,
  And Woden worship you and your victory,
  Hear, hear!

CYMEN.   Loki lacerate you for a liar
  And my foot in your teeth.

COLGRIN.   Quite so, exactly.

CYMEN. Wash my feet. Well, here's gut-comfort, anyway.
  Who can be called defeated who can still imbibe
  And belch?

CLODESUIDA. Defeated? Have you come back defeated
  When I sacrificed a good half-goat. . . .

CYMEN.   No doubt
  The wrong half, my jewel: the hind-quarters,
  And it brought us rumping home. Well,
  I'm still good enough for a bad joke.
  Liquor. Down the throat, sunshine; hum
  A lazy day to my inside. I'll doze
  In the meadow of my stomach. There's no warmth in a wife

CLODESUIDA. Who turns me cold? What besides defeat
  Have you still to tell me?

CYMEN.   Ask the dumb icebergs behind you.
  Take stock of those long jowls, my jewel,
  Those ruminating thundercoloured bulls
  Your brothers: and our pastry-pallid sons
  Who look on their father with such filial
  Disapproval. A fine resentful march
  This night has been, with no moon and no
  Conversation: nothing to break the monotony
  Except Tadfrid spitting once in every mile

And twenty-seven gurks from Osmer.
Spit some words at me instead, and gurk
Away your grudge. I'm tired of this subterranean
Muttering. Where's that water? My feet want comfort.

TADFRID. That's what this house will want before long, and may
Our guilt be forgiven us.

CLODESUIDA. What kind of talk is this?

CYMEN. Tell her, tell her. I'm humble.

CLODESUIDA. Do you say that?
Guilt, forgiveness, humility? What next?
Are you mad?

CYMEN. Tell her I am or you'll strangle yourselves
With an unspoken truth.

CLODESUIDA. Has none of you the courage
To speak?

TADFRID. Even though he's our overlord,
And though he may not at the time have been fully responsible—

OSMER. Let me tell her, Tadfrid; I speak faster.
It was approaching dusk, last evening.
We were catching a bright victory in our caps,
When Eccha, the earl, was killed by a thrust from the spear
Of this British brat:
And we were at the boy in the bat of an eye
To give him joy of our vengeance and a shove
To doom and a damned journey into dust,
When Cymen, our chief, our lord, your maleficent
Male—

CLODESUIDA. Though you're my brother I'll beat your mouth
If it passes a lie!

TADFRID. It's the truth that he says.

OSMER.   All right.
It's the truth that I say. Like a bear-sark blundering
He hit up our downcoming swords, sprang in
As white as a water-spout spinning in a full moon,
Shouting 'The gods can go and beg for blood!
Let 'em learn of us!'

TADFRID.   Word for word. 'Let 'em learn
Of us.'

CLODESUIDA. It's certain they heard!

OSMER.   From that moment, you
    could feel it,
The sky turned round, Ceaulin's men broke through,
Thor, in the scarlet dusk, swore and swung,
And Woden rode in rancour, as well he might,
And trod upon our dead.

TADFRID.   And so we slogged
Out from defeat, and he lugged the Briton with him.

CLODESUIDA. Is it believable?

CHELDRIC.   Look, father's weeping.

QUICHELM. A nice inheritance we have, all watermarked
With tears.

CLODESUIDA. Who's this man, spilling sawdust
Like an old puppet? I never saw him till now.
You make me ashamed, in front of our sons.

CYMEN.   Can't I
Have tears of rage? Why not the hot spout
Of indignation? Is it better to spew?
By the thousand and three thews of the muscular god,
Some fiend of this land came at my back!
I was thrown by a trick.

TADFRID. He should stand in the winter sea
Till his clothes freeze to his flesh. It's the only way
To be sure of a store of magic against such an evil.

CLODESUIDA. And catch death? That's an efficacious magic
If you like. It's more decently religious
To offer a sacrifice, than to offer himself
To an early grave.

OSMER. What devil was it that damned him
To its own design? Can he tell us that?

CYMEN. Some ancient
Damp god of this dooming island, who spat
The fungus out of his mouth and caught me napping.
I curse this kingdom, water, rock and soil!
I accuse and curse the creaking of its boughs
And the slaver on the mouth of its winds! It makes
A fool of me! Too many voices rasp
Out of decaying rafters, out of every cave
And every hole in the yellow sodden hills.
This is the golden future our fathers died for!
The gods look at it! Here's the slice of fortune
They came to carve with their courage
When they pitched themselves on the narrow, shuddering sea
To deal and duck death under the hanging chalk.
I stack my curses on those first rich rumours
Which fetched us here, rollicking with ambition.
I curse the muck and gravel where we walk.
I'd curse each singular soaking blade of grass
Except that a grey hair ties me for time.
Here we live, in our fathers' mirage.
Cities, they'd heard of, great with columns,
Gay cities, where wealth was bulging the doors
And the floors were sagging with the weight of gold.

The orchards rang with fruit, the hills moved
With grain like a lion's mane, and wherever
A river sauntered the fish swam, and eels
Reeled in bright mud. Flocks were fair,
And cows like pendulous fountains of alabaster
Went lowing over land where silver skulked
Waiting for skill; a land where summer days
Could call to one another across the night
Under the northern pole. So here we live
And choke in our father's mirage. Dreams they were,
As well we know; we live in the skull
Of the beautiful head which swam in the eyes of our fathers.
Our ploughshares jag on the stumps of moonwhite villas.
And my brain swerves with the sudden sting of one
Of the island gods, the down-and-out divinities
Moping, mildewed with immortality,
Cross-boned on weedy altars. I curse this land
That curses me!

OSMER.   Then cut yourself clear of its curse
And win this house again for Woden, before
We all know worse.
                    [*He drags forward* HOEL, *the Briton.*
                    Here's the land you loathe,
In bone and blood. Break its back.

CLODESUIDA.   We have always
Been god-fearing, but now it appears he fears
More gods than he knows what to do with. What can we do?

TADFRID. Obliterate the cause of sin. Do the undeed,
The death-lack which lost us our victory.
Where's the difficulty?

OSMER.   There is no difficulty.
Here's the quivering black-haired flesh,

As live as it was that time our blades were on him.
Well, we swing back on time, and hope the gods
Forget the indecision.

TADFRID.   It may seem now
To be somewhat in cold blood, but in fact his death
Was given to him in the battle yesterday;
This is merely the formal ceremony, which was overlooked.

QUICHELM. Kill him; make us respectable again.
I feel that all the gods are looking at us.

CHELDRIC. Do, father, kill him, as any other fellow's
Father would.

CLODESUIDA. Not inside the house!
The walls would never let his death go out.

CYMEN. No, nor anywhere here, I'll tell you all
Darker things yet. I have a great fear.

CLODESUIDA. Fear? Will you say that to the ears of your sons?

CYMEN. I say I fear myself, or rather
That not-myself which took my will,
Which forced a third strange eye into my head
So that I saw the world's dimensions altered.
I know no defence against that burst of fire.
[*To* HOEL.] You can tell me; what flogged away my strength,
What furtive power in your possession
Pulled the passion of my sword? Name that devil!
I'll have our gods harry him through the gaps
Between the stars, to where not even fiends
Can feed. Name him!

HOEL.   Who? Who am I to name?
I swear to God I know nothing of what you mean.

CYMEN. What God is that? You swear to a God?
What God?

HOEL. It was my grandfather who knew him well.
The One God, he's called. But I can't remember
The details; it's a long time ago that I saw
My grandfather, and I'm the last life
Of my family.

OSMER.   Send him where the moles
Can teach him to dig in the dark.

TADFRID.   His brows are marked
With the night already; douse the rest of him
And let's get to bed.

CYMEN.   Why shouldn't we give you the mercy
You showed to Eccha our earl?

HOEL.   It was all in the way
Of battle. I only expelled him from the world
As I let out my breath singing to the fame
Of Britain.

TADFRID. The fame of Britain! The fame of Britain
Is sung by us now. Let him echo Eccha
Into death, with the same ease.

OSMER.   Easy death,
Easy as shutting a door!

CYMEN.   This door shan't shut
Till I find what devil keeps it.

OSMER.   Then, by plague,
I'll void my vows of allegiance to this damned house!

TADFRID. And I; like a rat I'll run
Before the water rises.

CLODESUIDA.   Do you forget
Your wife and children? A sacrifice, Cymen,
This one sacrifice for our peace of mind.

CYMEN. What peace can we have until I know
  Whether or not the same misshapen fire again
  Will burn me? I've still got rags of reason
  To make our stark apprehension decent,
  And you shall be modest with me, or else bad-luck
  Will leer at the lot of us. If we kill him and bury him,
  I shall fill my lungs with relief and forget my fault
  And the flame will be on me while I whistle at a clear sky.
  No! This walking wound in my strength can walk on,
  Wake me in the morning, see me to my bed;
  He shall stand between me and the door so that his shadow
  Falls across everything I do: so every
  Moment shall have spears addressed to that dark
  Which lies in wait for my will. Alive,
  He's ours; dead, who knows to what
  Unfriendly power he will have given himself?
  Scowl at your own stampede of panic,
  Not at me. Look; the sun puts down
  The mist at last and looks out across the day.
  Here comes the burning sea of honey
  Over the grey sand of our defeat.
  We'll salute the sun that makes us men.
  Fill up the cups! [*To* COLGRIN.]
  O gigantic heart, beating in the breast of the sky,
  Lordlust the white-hot lion of the air,
  We are the men of the earth; our metal shouts
  With light only for you. (For chick's sake,
  Fill 'em up, fill 'em up!)—
  Give us huge harvest, potency and dominion.
  Make us pluck all from the teeth of this island.
  My strength comes back. By splendour,
  I'll send fear sprawling. By the zenith, I'll set
  My foot on the neck of the dark and get the gods

Again. [*He throws* HOEL *to the ground and puts his foot on his neck.*]
     Glory of life, I live!
We'll drink to our restored prosperity:
The sustaining sinews of tremendous Thor:
The unwearying, turbulent, blazing loins of Woden!
We raise our cups and drink, to the power of the gods,
This toast:

                    'Let us love one another.'
          [*His cup falls from his hand. He stands trembling.*

OSMER. What madness is this?

CLODESUIDA.   What words are these?

TADFRID.   He has fallen
     Foul of his brain again, protect us!

CHELDRIC.   'Let us
     What,' did father say?

QUICHELM.   'Love one another';
     What a way to honour the gods!

CLODESUIDA.   He's not himself.
     It's the patter of delirium he talks;
     A lack of sleep.

CYMEN.   I'm in good health!
     No-one shall excuse this fiend that twists my tongue,
     By saying I'm sick! Show, show, show,
     Devil! By the first yowl of the world's first babe
     I'll be the master of my own voice!
     Show! Come out of your secret place and let me
     See you climb to my sword. This time it means
     Death, your precious Briton's end, I kill him!
          [*He makes to kill* HOEL, *but his sword is against* QUIC-
          HELM.]

QUICHELM. Father!

CLODESUIDA.   No! Hold him! He's battle-blind.

OSMER. You madman, it's your son, Quichelm. What's
The matter? Here's the road you have to take,
The black-haired enemy. Turn here.

CYMEN.   It seems
All one, it seems all one. There's no distinction.
Which is my son?

QUICHELM.   Can't you see me?
I'm your son.

CYMEN.   And my enemy,
My own flesh. My sword knew you. Deny it:
My sword understood. Distinction has gone!

CLODESUIDA. Take him and make him sleep; it must be
The burning of his body. I'll not believe
He is mad. Get him to rest and sleep. Dip him
In sleep, that blue well where shadows walk
In water over their heads, and he'll be washed
Into reason. This has taken my strength, too.

CYMEN. All right, I'll sleep. I'll count myself as over
For a while. But let not you, not one of you,
Step between me and what's to come. This house
Is on my back; it goes my way. Dare nothing
Against the Briton, or dread will stay with you
Forever, like pock-marks. We'll master this mystery.
His death can keep; his death can wait for me.
        [*Exeunt* CLODESUIDA, CYMEN, QUICHELM, CHELDRIC.

OSMER. And we're kept jangling in the pocket of uncertainty
While Woden wonders how to spend us.

TADFRID.   And sleep
Will lay us open to all the supernatural riffraff

That ever came crawling out of cobwebs. Pleasant
Dreams.

OSMER [*to* COLGRIN]. Take him to the barn.
Hanging for you, if he escapes.

COLGRIN. A rope isn't my style. I haven't the neck for it.
                                        [*Exeunt* OSMER *and* TADFRID.

COLGRIN. Lowest form of life; that's you. Next to lowest, me.
So you can show respect. We'll make the barn
A guard-room. Get inside. This dizzy-dazzy
World made of morning sun and fog-spittle
Is nothing to do with you. Orders are otherwise.

HOEL. Try to think of it: I might by now
Have been wading about in the sway of death,
But I'm blinking at the light; my head swims with it.

COLGRIN. It doesn't do a man any good, daylight.
It means up and doing, and that means up to no good.
The best life is led horizontal
And absolutely unconscious. Get inside!
You flick of muck off the back hoof of a mule!
There's a point in being sworn at; it gives you something
To hand on to your fellow men. Now mind,
No monkey-tricks, no trying to escape,
I've got you covered—if I knew where I'd put my weapon.

HOEL. Where do you think I should escape to?

COLGRIN.   Why,
You'd skit off home.

HOEL.   That's where I've just escaped from
When I escaped death. Here I lie—
Hanging on to what was once my country,
Like an idiot clinging to the body of his dead mother.
Why don't you hack me off her? Why don't you?

Fool I was, fool I was, not to hug their swords
When they bore down on me. Why don't I settle
To a steady job in the grave, instead of this damned
Ambition for life, which doesn't even offer
A living wage? I want to live, even
If it's like a louse on the back of a sheep, skewering
Into the wool away from the beaks of crows;
Even like a limpet on a sour rock.
I want to live!

COLGRIN.   Me too;
Horizontal and absolutely unconscious.
But they keep us at it, they keep us at it.

                    Enter ANNA.

ANNA. Who at it? Not you at it. Don't you
Think he's ever at it; nobody's at it
Except old Anna. The farm's a hive
Of indolence: the place might as well be rubble.
Six upstanding men lying down, and nine
Cows lowing themselves into a cream cheese.
        [*She goes into the barn to take down the washing from where
        it hangs on* COLGRIN'S *sword stuck in a post.*
I won't say you're in my way
But I can't get to where I want to come to.

COLGRIN [*to* HOEL]. My only wife!

ANNA.   I'll take these into the sun.
Nothing ever dries in this country.

COLGRIN.   There's my weapon!
There's my dimpled sword! What do you mean, woman,
Hanging wet linen all over it? It's wrong
If it's rusty.

ANNA.   And a man is, too; and you're
So thick with rust you'd choke if you blew on yourself.

COLGRIN. I'm on special duty, Anna; I'm put to guard
A sad and savage Briton.

ANNA.   He needn't think
He'll be savage with me. He's caused a lot of trouble
Having to be conquered, and that's enough from him.
I shall probably get to be fond of him, but I'll never
Like him. It wouldn't be right if I did, when you think
Of all our men who've been killed killing these heathen.
And *this* isn't going to get the baby washed.

COLGRIN. What baby washed?

ANNA.   Can't I coin a phrase if I want to?
[*Exit* ANNA. *Enter* MARTINA *carrying an empty bowl.*

COLGRIN. My sword for a clothes-line!
Stand to attention. Here's my lord's daughter
Look as though you're working.

HOEL.   At what?

COLGRIN.   Here,
Plait some straw.

MARTINA.   Good morning, Colgrin.

COLGRIN.   Good-morning.
It's a bright day, lady, for the season.

MARTINA. Time, too. They made us wait for it.
I'm old with being young in a long winter.
I've almost forgotten how to walk on flowers.

COLGRIN. Everything would be all right if we'd been granted
Hibernation.

MARTINA.   We're not very favoured. The gods
Mean us to know they rule. Are your gods any
Kinder, Briton?

HOEL.   When I was a boy I was only
   Allowed to have one, though in that One, they said,
   There were three. But the altars are broken up. I've tried
   To pick away the moss to read the inscriptions
   But I've almost forgotten our language. I only know
   The god was both father and son and a brooding dove.

MARTINA. He's a Christian, Colgrin; and if you ask my mother
   She'll tell you that's worse than having no god at all.
   We have a Christian queen, though we try to keep it
   Dark, and in one of our prayers to the gods we say
   Give us our daily bread and forgive us our Queen.
   But we drove the Britons into the mountains; for years
   They've lain furtively in the setting sun,
   Those who live. Why aren't you lurking there, too?
   You should be crouching craven in a cave
   Warming your hands at the spark of your old god
   Who let you be conquered.

HOEL.   After my father was killed
   The Saxons kept me to work for them. My father
   Had always said What can one god do
   Against the many the invaders have?
   And he remembered earlier gods who still
   Harped on the hills, and hoped they would rally again.
   But they were too old. They only raised
   Infatuated echoes, and wept runnels.
   Then all the Britons were killed or fled, all
   Except my grandfather and my hip-high self.
   Him they kept for working metals which he did
   With his whole heart, forgetting the end of his race
   In a brooch design. He told me once
   How I'd been given in water to the One god.
   Soon afterwards he died, beating silver.

When I had grown the Saxons let me fight for them
And gave me a little freedom in exchange.

MARTINA. Enough for my father to take from you.
It's a pity
You had to be born a Briton. I'm forced to hate you.

HOEL. If I had been a Saxon . . .

MARTINA.   We should have killed you
To win your land, but considered you a brother.

COLGRIN. We should have killed you with consideration.
It isn't less fatal, of course, but it adds an air
Of glory, and we shake hands in Valhalla.

Enter CLODESUIDA.

CLODESUIDA. Martina, come, if you please! Two hands aren't
enough
To card and spin, and my brain goes with the wheel
Round and round in a horrible suspense.
What are you doing?

MARTINA.   Watching the herons. I'm coming.
They haunt the dregs of the mist like ghosts
Left on the yellow morning by a tide of sleep.

CLODESUIDA. Where did you take the bowl of meat?

MARTINA.   Where?

CLODESUIDA. I saw you come back from that old decaying
Tooth of a tower. And here's a string
Of bramble on your skirt, and burrs, and cleavers.
What were you doing there?

MARTINA.   I go very often.
Particularly when the house is overbearded
With splendid uncles.

CLODESUIDA.   Carrying a bowl of food?

MARTINA. Mother, I have to eat.

CLODESUIDA. Do you have to eat
Among bird-droppings and birds' bones and beaks
And owl-chawn mice and dead flies? Is that
Nicer than your uncles? The tower's a spitting-place
For all benighted life, a filthy ruin.
You have someone hidden there.

MARTINA. Suppose I have ...

CLODESUIDA. I do suppose you have; and I shall find who.
I wear myself out securing us to the gods
With every device that's orthodox, sacrificing
To the hour, to the split minute of the risen sun.
But how can I keep them kind if always
They're being displeased by the rest of you? It isn't
Easy to keep on the windy side of Woden
As anyone knows. Who have you hidden in the ruin?

MARTINA. Hardly anyone at all. A very old man:
Old enough to be his own grandfather.

CLODESUIDA. But why—

MARTINA. I dug him up. He was rather buried.
I found him in the quarry where it caved in.
His beard was twisted like mist in the roots of an oak-tree,
Beaded and bright with a slight rain, and he was crying
Like an old wet leaf. His hands were as brown as a nest
Of lizards, and his eyes were two pale stones
Dropping in a dark well. I thought I couldn't
Very well leave him where he was.

CLODESUIDA. You should
Have left him, until we could find out more about him.
Is he natural? Is he good or evil? Out of the quarry!
He might be as fatal as a toadstool.

MARTINA.   Maybe, maybe,
   Maybe. He comforts me.

CLODESUIDA.   He comforts you!
   In what way, comfortable? Now we come to it.
   What does he do?

MARTINA.   He screws up his eyes and looks
   At my hand and tells my future. It's better
   Than always having to placate the gods
   For fear something should happen. Besides, I like
   To know. He says, as far as he can remember,
   Though he has a terrible memory for names,
   His name is Merlin.

HOEL [*to* COLGRIN]. What did she say?

COLGRIN.   She said
   I was so thick with rust I'd choke if I blew.
   My sword for a clothes-line!

HOEL.   Merlin!

CLODESUIDA.   I only hope
   He has done no harm to us yet, whatever he is,
   Whatever his tongue clinks at, sitting with the rats.
   It's no good having gods at the door if there
   Are devils on the hearth. Your uncles, one or both,
   Shall see him.

HOEL.   She calls him Merlin. She has caught
   An echo that booms in the deepest cave of my race
   And brings it here, out into the winter light!

MARTINA. You shall see him for yourself.
   Here he comes, with the red earth still on him
   And his beard springing surprises on the breeze.
   He promised not to break his hiding. Well,
   You see how old he is. And how confused in the sun.
   With two days' growth of shadow from the tower.

Enter MERLIN.

You've broken faith. You promised you'd lie low.

[MERLIN *moves on towards* HOEL.

CLODESUIDA. What is he after?

MERLIN [*to* HOEL].   Ail i'r ar ael Eryri
Cyfartal hoewal a hi. Ar oror wir arwa.

HOEL. Peth yw . . . peth yw . . . I can't remember
How to speak. I use the words of the Saxons.

CLODESUIDA. Another heathen! Did you know he was a Briton?
Is that why you hid him from me?

MERLIN [*to* HOEL].   A British voice.
It breaks a fast of years; I roll you
Wonderfully on my tongue. I was half asleep
But I heard you. This wide harp of winter
Reverberates. I had stupidly imagined
The human landscape had left me for ever.
The face of the foam for me (I told myself)
Until I die. All your expectation
Of friendship, old man (I said to myself)
Is a wink from the eye of a bullfinch
Or the slower solemnities of a tortoise
Or a grudging goodnight from the dark lungs of a toad.
And then your voice alights on my ear. I bless you
From the bottom of my slowly budding grave.

CLODESUIDA. You must speak to my brothers before we let you
wander
All over our land.

HOEL.   Madam, this may be Merlin.
Still Merlin. Do you understand?

MERLIN. You are surprised, I see, to find me still
Giving and taking the air. You think I should long ago

Have sunk to the golden bed of the troubled river.
But I have obstreperous garments that keep me floating.
I merely float, in a desultory, though
Delighted, kind of way. And my garments begin
To be heavy. Presently, on the surface of life,
You may observe a doting bubble, smiling
Inanely at the sun until it dissolves,
And then you'll know the time has been.

HOEL.   It has gone
Already for us. We're lost and scattered.

MERLIN.   Be lost
And then be found. It's an old custom of the earth
From year to year. I could do something;
But I lost my trumpet of zeal when Arthur died
And now I only wind a grey note
Of memory, and the hills are quiet.

CLODESUIDA.   Did you hear
What I said to you?

MARTINA.   Father has come from the house.

Enter CYMEN.

CLODESUIDA. Oh, you should be sleeping.

CYMEN.   No sleep came.
An occasional shadow across my bed from a cloud
Of weariness, but the glare of the brain persisted.
Where is the Briton?

CLODESUIDA.   There in the barn, there,
Talking to an old man of his tribe, or an old
Sorcerer, or some brewer of trouble.
We should rid the country of these things which aren't ourselves.

CYMEN. Rid the brain of uncertainty, rid the heart
  Of its fear.

> [*He goes to the barn.*

      How did this old man come here?
The kingdom has been scoured of you islanders.
What are you hanging about for?

MERLIN.   I pluck at my roots
  But they won't be fetched away from a world which possesses me
  Like an unforgettable woman who was once my own.
  I walk on the earth, besotted by her, waiting
  To bring to her the devotion of my dust.

HOEL.   It's Merlin. He's still among us.

CYMEN.   What is he?
  Is it one of your superstitions,
  A damned invention of the air? Tell me
  What your existence is or, by the night,
  I'll ask your flesh with a sharper edge to the question
  Come on, now; are you superannuated god
  Or working devil, or mere entangled man?

MERLIN. No god, I hope; that would take too much
  Endurance. Whatever man may be
  I am that thing, though my birth, I've been given to believe,
  Had some darkness in it. But then, which of us
  Can say he is altogether free of a strain
  Of hell in his blood? My father could be called
  Pure man, if such a thing existed.

CYMEN.   Then
  What powers pursue us here? You know this island
  Thoroughly. Parade your spirits, good
  And bad, and I'll identify the mischief!

CLODESUIDA Will you ask *them*, men of the race
We conquered?

MARTINA.   Ask the prisoner
If he isn't a Christian. He's a godless Christian
Even if he can't remember.

CLODESUIDA.   Why can't we get rid of them
Once and for all? The gods will strike at them
And everyone knows how carelessly they aim. The blow
May fall on us.

COLGRIN.   Colgrin will catch it, Colgrin
Is sure to catch it. The rest of the world will dodge
And I shall be in the way.

CYMEN.   I'll ask the louse
In the filthy shirt of a corpse in the bottom of a ditch
If I can learn what it is I've learnt to dread.
I lay on my bed and felt it stand with its feet
Planted on either side of my heart, and I looked
Up the tower of its body to find the face
To know if it meant to help or hinder,
But it was blotted out by a shield of thunder.
Am I to sacrifice without end and then
Be given no peace? The skirts of the gods
Drag in our mud. We feel the touch
And take it to be a kiss. But they see we soil them
And twitch themselves away. Name to me
What mocked me with a mood of mercy and therefore
Defeat. Who desired that?

MERLIN.   Who, apart
From ourselves, can see any difference between
Our victories and our defeats, dear sir?
Not beast, nor bird, nor even the anticipating
Vulture watching for the battle's end,

Nor a single mile of devoted dispassionate ground.
All indifferent. Much more so your gods
Who live without the world, who never feel
As the world feels in springtime the stab of the spear
And the spurt of golden blood,
Winter's wound-in-the-side, the place where life begins.
Nothing, it seems, cares for your defeat.

CLODESUIDA. How did I say these Britons would answer you?
It shames us to stand and listen. Didn't we conquer them?

MERLIN. Quest and conquest and quest again. It might well
Make you fretful if you weren't expecting it.

CYMEN. You are conquered. Both you or this boy
I can destroy now, and no questions asked.

MERLIN. Death is what conquers the killer, not the killed.
How pleasant it is to talk, even
In your language. I have a way—your daughter
May have told you—of looking ahead, having made
My peace with Time, at some expense to my soul.
It's curious to know that in the course
Of the movement of years which wears away distinction,
You, and moreover your conquerors, will bear
Kindly and as though by nature our name, the British
Name, and all the paraphernalia, legend
And history, as though you were our widow
Not our conqueror. And well may the weeds become you.

CYMEN. You're a hideous old wiseacre
Of sheepbitten kale. But give me an answer.
If, as you imagine, our gods have no care
Whether we win or lose, what cuckoo power
Is it that usurps the nest of my soul?

MERLIN. You ask an old pagan? Old Merlin, old
Eternal suckling, who cannot drag his lips

Away from the breast of the earth, even to grow
Into the maturity of heaven. Nothing can wean him
Until his mother puts upon her nipple
The vinegar of death, though, when I walked
Between the dog-rose hedges of my manhood,
It was in a Christian land: in Arthur's land.
There I gleamed in the iris of creation's
Eye, and there I laughed as a man should,
Between the pillars of my ribs in the wide
Nave of my chest. A Christian land. There
It was, and old Joseph's faithful staff
Breaking into scarlet bud in the falling snow.
But, as I said at the time, the miracle
Was commonplace: staves of chestnut wood
And maywood and the like perform it every year.
And men broke their swords in the love of battle,
And broke their hearts in the love of women,
And broke the holy bread in the love of God.
I saw them ride away between their loves
Into a circle of the snow-white wind
And so into my head's old yellow world
Of bone.

CYMEN.   Your Christian land was weak, it shook
Down, it burnt, its ash was blown
Into our food and drink. What I'm inflicted with
Is strong, destroying me with a cry of love,
A violence of humility arrogantly
Demanding all I am or possess or have ambitions for,
Insistent as a tocsin which was sounded
When the sun first caught on fire, and ever since
Clangs alarm with a steady beat in the wild
Night of history. This doesn't come

From the watery light of what you think you remember.
A lashing logic drags me away from my gods.
Let it face me like a man!

MERLIN.   It may be already
This power has faced you like a man, on a certain
Century's peak from which the circling low land
Is, to eternity, surveyed. Still, still,
Earth winds delicious arms; it isn't strange
Our human eyes should close upon her, like a flower
Closing on a globe of dew, and wish to see
Nothing but this. And here am I
Doting into oblivion.

CLODESUIDA.   Send him off,
With his ancient ramifications; go to sleep
And be well.

CYMEN [*to* HOEL]. Do I have to come to you again?
You, a speck of the dust which three of our generations
Have marched over: what light flung from you
To me? Why did my strength startle from your
Futility?

HOEL.   On my soul, I've done nothing against you
Except to make war. I've known nothing except
Your mercy; that indeed was a kind of light to me.
I want to live, having a life in me
Which seems to demand it.

MERLIN.   Having a death in him, too:
That death by drowning in the river of his baptism
From which he rose a dripping Christian child
In a land which had become a grave to us all,
Though in that grave of Britain old Merlin, for one,
Was happy enough because he could hold, both hill

And valley, his leafy love in his arms,
Old pagan that he is.

HOEL.   The weather of twenty
Years has blown me dry, and long lost me
All the charms I ever had of that.

MERLIN. The spirit is very tenacious of such water.

CYMEN. The spirit again! You nod and look beyond me,
And pretend to know nothing. Do you dare to say
The world has a secret direction passing the gods?
And does it run through me? [*To* CLODESUIDA.] Take me from
   them.
I'm mad, mad to talk to the slaves.

CLODESUIDA.   Rest, Cymen.

CYMEN. I am alive and so there is no rest.

CLODESUIDA. It's you who churn up the air; the air itself
Is as unruffled as ever. Trust our gods
And put these heathen to work.

                    Enter ANNA.

ANNA.   Master, master, master!
Where is the master? The wolves, the savages!
An old woman's no use! Oh, the master!

CYMEN. What's the matter?

ANNA.   So many wolves, the fields
Are a bear-garden—ma'am, your brothers!—grey,
Snarling, vicious, a terrible pack—they're into
The sheep!

CYMEN.   The sheep!

CLODESUIDA.   Brothers, help, help us,
Wake, the wolves have come!

ANNA.   The sheep and the lambs,
  All we have!

MARTINA.   In the daylight, in daylight, too!
  What could have brought them?

ANNA.   Why, hunger, hunger, the appetite,
  The spite of the belly!

      Enter TADFRID, OSMER, QUICHELM, *and* CHELDRIC.

OSMER.   What's the cry?

CLODESUIDA.   The wolves!
  They're falling on the flock!

TADFRID.   So it begins,
  Bad-luck already.

OSMER.   Down to them, then, and save
  What's still for saving.
          [CYMEN *has already snatched* COLGRIN'S *sword and gone;*
          HOEL *also, ahead of him. Now the rest follow, shouting to
          scatter the wolves.*

ANNA.   I'm fit for nothing now
  But whisking eggs, I'm trembling so.
  Why should such things be? Such fangs, I have
  Sharp pains in the back just to have seen them
  Gnashing in the light. [*Seeing* COLGRIN]: Why are you here,
  You, taking up space as though time didn't begin
  Until the day after to-morrow? Do all legs move
  Except the two that keep the ground away from you?
  Why don't you go and help?

COLGRIN.   My dear, good woman,
  I'm here on duty.

ANNA.   What duty would you mean,
  I wonder? The prisoner's gone.

COLGRIN.   All the more reason
  Why the other half of the arrangement should stand.
  If the horse gets out of the stable it doesn't mean
  The stable is justified in following.
  I'm a man who can be relied on.

ANNA.   So you are.
  Well, at least when your time comes to be buried
  They'll have no trouble keeping you under the ground.
  But why should wolves be set upon us? Men
  Make enough misfortunes for themselves, without
  Natural calamities happening as well.
  The old gentleman agrees.

MERLIN.   Considerable
  Age makes me nod; I neither agree
  Nor disagree. I'm too near-sighted now
  To be able to distinguish one thing from another,
  The storm-swollen river from the tear-swollen eyes,
  Or the bare cracked earth from the burnt-out face,
  Or the forest soughing from the sighing heart.
  What is in one is in the other, a mood
  Of rage which turns upon itself to savage
  Its own body, since there's nothing except itself
  On which anger can alight; it sinks into time
  Like a sword into snow
  And the roots receive all weathers and subsist,
  And the seasons are reconciled. When, years ago,
  The Romans fell away from our branching roads
  Like brazen leaves, answering
  The hopeless windy trumpets from their home,
  Your tribes waged winter upon us, till our limbs
  Ached with the carving cold. You blackened
  The veins of the valleys with our dried blood. And at last

Your lives croaked like crows on a dead bough
And the echoes clanged against you. But I can hear
Faintly on the twittering sea a sail
Moving greatly where the waves, like harvest-home,
Come hugely on our coast: the men of Rome
Returning, bringing God, winter over, a breath
Of green exhaled from the hedges, the wall of sky
Breached by larksong. Primrose and violet
And all frail privileges of the early ground
Gather like pilgrims in the aisles of the sun.
A ship in full foliage rides in
Over the February foam, and rests
Upon Britain.

COLGRIN.   He's in the clouds, you see; he's away
On his own; he's blowing about like the hairs in his beard.

ANNA. Maybe, yes, and maybe also his beard
Has caught on something. He seems to have brought
The other side of the hill into his head.
It's good to see—we anticipate little enough—
And certainly to-day, I noticed myself,
Winter is wearing thin; it's beginning to show
The flowering body through.

COLGRIN.   It's a hard time,
The spring; it makes me lose all my energy.

Enter CLODESUIDA.

CLODESUIDA. Did you see it, did ever your eyes? He must be as
  wild
As an animal in his heart! Who ever saw
Such wrestling between hand and claw?

ANNA.   Such what,
Such wrestling? I hadn't hard enough eyes

To put them again on those poor bleating lambs.
Are the wolves away now? Are the wolves away?
I still shake for the sake of those sheep.

CLODESUIDA.   The wolves
Are beaten off. But the Briton killed the grimmest,
The greatest: with his hands, with his hands as bare
As mine: met and mauled the scavenger, with a grip
Under the blood and froth of the jaws, he shook
And choked the howling out of its fangs
And forced it to a carcase. It was horror
And hope and terror and triumph to see it.

ANNA. The boy? The Briton? with bare hands?

MERLIN.   Like a shepherd
With a lion.

COLGRIN.   With his bare hands?

ANNA.   It's just as well
To hang the wet linen on your sword,
You heavy hero on my conscience.

        Enter TADFRID, OSMER, QUICHELM, *and* CHELDRIC.

CLODESUIDA.   It's a tale
I'll tell to my grave! My heart is hammering
And still hugging the fearful sport of the struggle.
What shall we do to reward him?

OSMER.   Reward him? his death
Can reward him. Who's the fool who's going to kiss
Future trouble? Who does, deserves to lie
With the grass growing up through a crack in the skull.

CLODESUIDA. What do you mean? Didn't he enlist himself
Against our disaster?

TADFRID.   But in what power's name?
Osmer fears—

OSMER.   And very properly fears.
I'm not quite a child in this cleft-stick of life.

Enter CYMEN.

CYMEN. Are you still rolling your marbles of thunder?
I hear what you say. Still breaking wind to make
A hurricane. I am very tired.

OSMER.   And so
Are we all with anxiety. And so no doubt
Are the crouching gods who contain their final leap
Waiting for wisdom from us.

TADFRID.   And not holding
For long, now that the first roar has come.

CYMEN. That may be. I know well enough
The weight of the silence that's on our shoulders now.
I move under it like the moving mole
That raises the hackles of dead leaves.
Under me, silence; round me, silence, air,
The wind hushing the world to hear
The wind hushing the world; and over me,
Silence upon silence upon silence,
Unuttering vapour, unutterable void.
What do you want me to do?

OSMER.   Make retribution
Before we're godsmitten again.

TADFRID.   A sacrifice.

OSMER. The only possible sacrifice, the Briton.

CLODESUIDA. Can they be right, Cymen? Certainly
We must do what is necessary, though when
I saw the wolf destroyed—

OSMER.   As now you shall see
Our luck's neck fractured, unless we act.

D

The Briton sprang on the back of a punishment
Justly put upon us by the gods.

TADFRID. That's so. And by what muscle, except a devil's,
Could he elbow himself between our gods and us?

OSMER. It's perfectly proper that we should contest our punish-
ment,
If we can. The gods relish a knock or two
Before they lean back and insist on being
Propitiated. But by no right does this Briton
Break in and ruffle them beyond all hope.
His demon rams him to it to make our world
The worse for us.

QUICHELM.   We've got to be free of him.
Cut him to quiet. He's a flint that's going to skag us.
Hit the spark of life out of him, father.

TADFRID. What else but a power of the dark would send him
Scudding into the teeth and talons
Of a probable death, for us, his enemies?
If you let him live among us—

> [*Enter* HOEL, *helped by* MARTINA. *His shoulders have been
> clawed by the wolf. They walk across to the barn, watched in
> silence by the others.*

CYMEN.   I will sacrifice.

OSMER. Then back we come to easy breathing
And a chance of pleasure.

CLODESUIDA.   Let me think of the harm
He would do us, his brain's blackened teeth,
And not sicken at his killing. What the gods
Want we'll give them, even though our blood
Freezes.

CYMEN. I will sacrifice.
  I'll pay off whatever dark debts there are
  And come to the morning, square. I am tired, tired
  Of being ground between the staring stones
  Of air and earth. I'll satisfy the silence.
  ·Bring me one of the white goats.

TADFRID *and* OSMER.   A goat?

CYMEN. One silence of death is as deep as another
  To satisfy the silence. It will do
  To patch wherever a whisper from above
  Can still creep out. Bring me the goat.

CLODESUIDA.   But this
  Can't please them if they demand the Briton?

OSMER. It's livestock thrown away.

TADFRID.   Look, he goes
  To pray to them.

CYMEN [*at the altar*]. Gods, our gods, gods
  Of the long forced-march of our blood's generations
  Dead and living. Goaders, grappling gods,
  Whose iron feet pace on thunder's floor
  Up and down in the hall where chaos groaned
  And bore creation sobbing. Boding gods,
  Who broad in the universe consume our days
  Like food, and crunch us, good and bad,
  Like bones. What do I do by sacrifice?
  The blood flows, the ground soaks it up,
  The poisoned nightshade grows, the fears go on,
  The dread of doom gropes into the bowels,
  And hope, with her ambitious shovel, sweats
  To dig the pit which swallows us at last.
  The sacrifice is despair and desperation!

The deed of death is done and done and always
To do, death and death and death; and still
We cannot come and stand between your knees.
Why? By what stroke was the human flesh
Hacked so separate from the body of life
Beyond us? You make us to be the eternal alien
In our own world. Then I submit. Separation
To separation! Dedicated stones
Can lie asunder until the break is joined!

> [CYMEN *throws down the stones of the altar. The rest, except*
> HOEL, *throw themselves in horror on to the ground.*

Answer, then, answer! I am alone, without hope.
The outlaw, no longer the groveller on the knee.
Silence me! Come down and silence me!
Then at least I shall have some kind of part
With all the rest.

> [*They wait.*]

Not even that?
Is separation between man and gods
So complete? Can't you even bring me to silence?

> [*A voice from a short way off is heard calling 'Cymen!*
> *Cymen of the Copse!' CYMEN stands startled. The rest raise*
> *themselves partly from the ground in apprehension. The voice*
> *calls, again, nearer.*

CYMEN. What is it? Who is it? I am here on my ground.

> *Enter a* MESSENGER.

MESSENGER. Cymen of the Copse, is he here?

CYMEN.   I'm that man.

MESSENGER. You're summoned to the general assemblage
   Of all householders, copyholders, smallholders, and tenant-
      farmers,
   At the command of Ethelbert, lord and king of Kent,

To receive the person and words of Augustine
Exponent of the Christian god.
Proper precautions are being taken, and all
Provision made, to protect each person present
From being taken at a disadvantage
By the craft of any spirit whatsoever,
Evil or good. Therefore you will take your stand
Not under the king's roof
But where the air keeps open house
And the sun in the sky suffers all for all,
Or at least if any charms are set afoot
They will be less concentrated, owing to the wind.

CYMEN. Am I called to the king?

MESSENGER.   You assemble on the western hill
To receive the person and words—

MERLIN.   Of Augustine
Sent by Gregory of Rome who on a market-day
Saw angels where we see our enemies.

ANNA. He knew, that's what he said, he saw them coming
In a ship full of primroses from Rome!

CYMEN [*to the* MESSENGER]. I am slow to understand you. I was
up
On the bare back of dreadful thoughts. Who chose
That you should come to me now? What ground
Am I dismounting onto, your ordinary summons
To the king?

MESSENGER. You find it unpleasant? The news, I see,
Has reached you already, and distaste, I suppose,
Is understandable, though all you're supposed to do
Is to sit and give the appearance of paying attention
Out of consideration for the queen.

CLODESUIDA. She would like to make heathen of us all!
  We're on poor enough terms with the gods as it is
  Without seeming to keep open minds.

OSMER.   They're only
  Hesitating over the choice of weapons
  They mean to use against us.

TADFRID.   The sky is clear,
  The sun still shines, but there's little doubt
  Their indignation is mounting under the self-control
  Of the horizon. Let the king indulge the queen
  If it keeps her wife-minded, but here more than ever
  We've got to remain rigid with reality.

MESSENGER. In my opinion you're taking devoutness too hard.
  The gods won't object to our being a bit diplomatic.
  I'll leave you to make your way, Cymen of the Copse.

CYMEN. Time makes my way, and I go on with time.
  What is contrives what will be. Yes, I shall come.

                              [*Exit the* MESSENGER.

TADFRID. Will you go and leave us now to suffer
  In whatever suffering comes of your blasphemy?

OSMER. Let him go.

CLODESUIDA.   But now of all times isn't the time;
  He's so wretched from his brainstorm of wrong,
  Every pore of his skin's wide open to punishment.

OSMER. Let him go, let him go.

CYMEN [*to* HOEL].   Your god has come, perhaps,
  Or lies in wait on the lips of a man from Rome.
  Strange. As though a spirit in you, like
  A wild fowl hiding in the mere of your flesh,
  Heard the sound far off and flew up clamouring
  Rousing a spirit in me. We're in the path

Of change. And I must go to meet the change,
Being unable to live unaltered.

HOEL.   Is it true,
Indeed? Is the One god making his way again
In through the many?

CYMEN.   I go to know.
I go to dare my arm into the thicket
To know what lifts its head there, whether rose
Or tiger, or tiger and rose together.
Be undisturbed, my dear disturbed wife.
If I rock, it's with the rocking of the world;
It will get me to sleep in time. As for the rest of you,
Wait, with a certain degree of trust.
Yes, you can build up the altar again if you must.
It will be somewhere to sit when the days are warmer.
Meanwhile, the silence keep you, the silence
Be gracious unto you and give you peace.

> [*Exit* CYMEN. TADFRID *and* OSMER *have started, and now
> continue, to rebuild the altar.* CLODESUIDA *watches* CYMEN
> *on his way.*

CLODESUIDA. Should he go? He walks steadily enough now,
Very much as he does behind a plough. Is this only
A lull on his brain? Can he avoid trouble
After what he has done?

TADFRID.   The air is clearer without him.
And let's hope the bloodshot eyes above us
Have followed him and don't still fix on us here.

QUICHELM. It was awful to watch him. We must make it right with
    the gods.
They can't expect sons to carry the blame for fathers.
Would they make us suffer because of our blood?

HOEL.   Yes;
  Or from whose example would men have learnt that trick?

OSMER. You'll scream yourself sorry if we turn ourselves to you.

MARTINA [*to* HOEL]. You're still a Briton, even though I have
  Washed your wounds. Lie low, and don't make trouble.

CHELDRIC. Our mother's blood flows in us too, uncle,
  And mother fears the gods. Won't that be taken
  Into account?

CLODESUIDA. The same with the gods as with men;
  Women are only camp-followers, they take
  Our obedience for granted. If *we* blasphemed
  They would pinch our cheeks and resume the course of history
  As though nothing had happened. We succeed or suffer
  According to our men.

ANNA.   Then I roughen my hands
  For a fine lark.

CLODESUIDA. Day's work is still to do,
  Whatever the day's doom. I have no hope
  To be able to know what hope to have. My hands
  Can only draw their everyday conclusions.

ANNA. Yes, we must busy ourselves, and try to forget
  The complication of what's up there beyond us.
  [*To* COLGRIN.] Are you still rooted to the spot with duty?

COLGRIN. Unavoidably static.

OSMER.   Get onto your work.

COLGRIN. But suppose the prisoner—

OSMER.   Suppose
  You do what you're told and quick.

COLGRIN.   Quick? I'll suppose
  Anything once; but that's not how I am.
  I was born midway between the quick and the dead.

ANNA. Budge over a little farther from the grave.
            [*Exeunt* CLODESUIDA, COLGRIN, *and* ANNA.

TADFRID. What do we mean to do? The altar stones
    Now stand as they were. But not to them.
    To them the stones are still pitching and blundering
    From jutting god to jutting god, down
    The scowling scarp of their everlasting memory.
    They say the gods were formed
    Out of the old hurt pride of rejected chaos
    Which is still lusting for the body of the world we walk on.

OSMER. If they'll give us time and the merest shove
    In the lucky direction we're leaning to already,
    We shall be able to elude the allegiance to Cymen
    Which is such an obstacle in the way of well-doing,
    Nullify guilt and mollify the gods
    And bury the brat's guts for good in the ground.
    You shall see; it will be as I say
    If the gods give us time.

TADFRID.   But Cymen claimed
    His death to himself.

OSMER.   We'll do it in his name;
    If a moment which insists on action
    Comes while he's away, he would expect us
    To live the moment for him.

TADFRID.   If the crisis came.

QUICHELM. What's the talk? Do you think we're in for the worst?
    Do you see any hope that we can relax
    Now that father's gone, or what's your guess?

CHELDRIC. Isn't the danger less?

OSMER.   Come away from here.
    I've got a screw of courage you can chew;

We're not committed to damnation yet.
Let your sister stay. We'll pray, with a certain purpose.
        [*Exeunt* TADFRID, OSMER, QUICHELM, *and* CHELDRIC.

MARTINA. They hate you; and that's easy to understand.
    We have existence on such hard terms,
    As though birth into the world had been a favour
    Instantly regretted. We haven't the air
    To spare for strangers. I hope the claw-marks heal.
    I've done my best for them.

HOEL.   Thanks. Are you going in?

MARTINA. Of course. There's nothing to keep me here.

HOEL. No; there's nothing.

MARTINA.   What do you want?

HOEL.   I wonder
    What it was that came and wielded your father and left me
    Alive?

MARTINA. I'll not worry about my father,
    Nor my mother, nor my uncles nor, between ourselves,
    The gods. The universe is too ill-fitting
    And large. I am very careful about small
    Things, such as wearing green in the third month
    Or bringing blackthorn under the roof;
    But the big things, such as gods, must look after themselves.

HOEL. Still, I'm curious about the One god.
    I've never completely shaken him off. He seems
    To insist.

MARTINA. You're a born heathen. Get some sleep.
    You look too tired to be hated
    And that won't do at all.

HOEL.   Do you have to hate me?

MARTINA. It isn't one of my easiest duties. But how else
   Can we keep our footing or our self-esteem?
   Now sleep and look malignant when you wake.

HOEL. Sleep, yes. My fields need rain. Sleep
   Can drench down and welcome.
                    [*Exit* MARTINA. HOEL *lies in the straw and sleeps.*

MERLIN.   Welcome, sleep;
   Welcome into the winter head of the world
   The sleep of Spring, which grows dreams,
   Nodding trumpets, blowing bells,
   A jingle of birds whenever the sun moves,
   Never so lightly; all dreams,
   All dreams out of slumbering rock:
   Lambs in a skittle prance, the hobbling rook
   Like a witch picking sticks,
   And pinnacle-ears the hare
   Ladling himself along in the emerald wheat:
   All dreams out of the slumbering rock,
   Each dream answering to a shape
   Which was in dream before the shapes were shapen;
   Each growing obediently to a form,
   To its own sound, shrill or deep, to a life
   In water or air, in light or night or mould;
   By sense or thread perceiving,
   Eye, tendril, nostril, ear; to the shape of the dream
   In the ancient slumbering rock.
   And above the shapes of life, the shape
   Of death, the singular shape of the dream dissolving,
   Into which all obediently come.
   And above the shape of death, the shape of the will
   Of the slumbering rock, the end of the throes of sleep
   Where the stream of the dream wakes in the open eyes

Of the sea of the love of the morning of the God.
Here's an old man whiling away a spring
Day, with thoughts so far beyond the moss
He roots in, they're as nebulous
As the muted flute of a dove to the root of a tree.
Never mind. However warmly I curl
My tail around my feet and admire myself
Reflected in the nut before I bite,
Still I observe the very obdurate pressure
Edging men towards a shape beyond
The shape they know. Now and then, by a spurt
Of light, they manage the clumsy approximation,
Overturn it, turn again, refashion
Nearer the advising of their need.
Always the shape lying over the life.
Pattern of worm in the sand was not the shape,
Nor the booming body of enormous beast,
Nor the spread fan of the blue-eyed quivering tail,
Nor the weave of the nest, nor the spun wheel of the web,
Nor the maze and cellarage of honey, nor
The charts and maps of men. The shape shone
Like a faint circle round a moon
Of hazy gods, and age by age
The gods reformed according to the shape,
According to the shape that was a word,
According to Thy Word. Here's more than half
A pagan whiling away the spring sunshine.
The morning has come within a distant sight
Of evening, and the wandering shadows begin
To stretch their limbs a little. I shall move
Myself, into the quiet of the tumbling tower,
For an hour or two of casual obliteration
And break more ground for dreams.

[*Exit* MERLIN. *Enter, after a pause,* MARTINA *with a bowl of food. She goes to* HOEL, *who is still asleep.*

MARTINA. You're even less of an enemy when you sleep.
Wake up. You've gone where we're all of one size.
Bring yourself back and know your station.

HOEL.   Yes?
This isn't where I sleep. Why is my heart
So heavy?

MARTINA. Here is food. You have to be
A good enemy and eat.

HOEL.   You went indoors.
I thought you might not come back again.

MARTINA. Aren't you hungry?

HOEL.   Perhaps. From where I sit
On the kerb of sleep I feel I know you better
Than I did before. Take the bowl in your hands
And let me eat the food from there.

MARTINA. Am I your servant?

HOEL.   I'm your servant. I slept
When you said sleep, and I'll eat like a tame swan
Out of your hands.

MARTINA.   Too black for a swan,
You'd make me a good shadow. I'll ask my father
To give you to be my personal shadow,
To walk behind me in the morning, and before me
In the evening, and at noon I'll have you
Under my feet.

HOEL.   I shall adjust myself
Easily to noon.

MARTINA.   You'll feel humiliated
And bite the dust.

HOEL.   I shall feel delighted
And kiss the sole of your foot.

MARTINA.   It's clear you're nothing
But a poor-spirited Briton if you're willing
To become a girl's shadow.

HOEL.   Yes, indeed;
A poor-spirited Briton; you remind me
In good time.

MARTINA.   But a Briton who, if he were a Jute,
Would be brave and agreeable. So be glad of that.

HOEL. What simple-witted things the affections are,
That can't perceive whether people are enemies
Or friends. You would think the strong distinction
Between race and race would be clear even to the heart
Though it does lie so retired
Beating its time away in the human breast.

MARTINA. You talk of nothing that interests me. Eat
Your food.

        Enter TADFRID, OSMER, QUICHELM, *and* CHELDRIC.

OSMER.   You see, she has gone to him again.
It's the way I said it would be. His damned contagion
Spreads.

TADFRID. It flies first to the weakest place.
That girl sees nothing but an eye and a mouth
And doesn't care.

QUICHELM.   She can go and eat grass
Before I call her sister again.

OSMER.   She gives us
The grounds for getting him where the gods want him.
He is ours and his blood's as good as gone to them.

If we hesitated now even Cymen would say
We were as puny as pulp.

MARTINA [*to* HOEL].   You look so sad.

[*She kisses him on the forehead.*

QUICHELM [*leaping forward*]. Leper-flesh!

CHELDRIC.   He snared her!

MARTINA.   What's so wrong?

QUICHELM. You and the flicker of your rutting eyes are wrong!

OSMER. Toleration has gone to the limit. Now
We strike. You black pawn of the devil's game,
Come out.

HOEL.   Why, what is it you mean to do?

OSMER. Make much of you, make a god's meal of you,
And make our peace with you, with you as peacemaker,
And not too soon. It's a quiet future for you.
I said come out.

MARTINA.   No! My father said he was not to be harmed!

OSMER. He wouldn't say it now. Uncertainty
Has dandled us enough to make us sick
For life. Now we're not going to fob
The gods off any longer.

QUICHELM.   Must we wait?
Give me the word, and I'll fetch his cringing carcase
Out for you.

MARTINA.   Don't dare to touch him!

TADFRID.   Niece,
We must submit to the wish of what we worship.
We rid the world of an evil. Let's not rage.
We do what's demanded of us, with solemnity,
Without passion. Fetch him out.

MARTINA.   No, you shall not!

OSMER. Take her!
> [CHELDRIC *drags back* MARTINA *and holds her.* OSMER
> *and* QUICHELM *fetch* HOEL *to the centre of the stage.*

MARTINA.   Cowards!

HOEL.   Let me live, do, do
Let me live.

TADFRID. Bring him to the tree; we'll offer him
In Woden's way, the Woden death. Come on;
We'll be well out of our fear.

MARTINA.   Cowards, cowards,
Cowards, sneakthieves, only dare with father gone!
> [*They fasten him to the tree with his arms spread.*

HOEL. Is this the end indeed? Where now for me?

MARTINA. Father! Father!

HOEL.   Son and the brooding dove.
Call him again.

MARTINA.   Father!

OSMER.   We set this house
Free from fear and guilt and the working of darkness.

QUICHELM. We clean our hearts.

TADFRID.   The sun flows on the spear.
The spear answers the sun. They are one, and go
To the act in the concord of a sacrifice.

HOEL. Death, be to me like a hand that shades
My eyes, helping me to see
Into the light.

OSMER. Woden, we pay your dues
Of blood.

TADFRID. Receive it and receive us back
Into a comfortable security.
[OSMER *makes to plunge the spear.* MARTINA *breaks free of*
CHELDRIC *and crying 'No!' tries to prevent the stroke.*
[*Enter* CLODESUIDA.

CLODESUIDA. Have they struck at us again, the gods?
What more
Have we to bear?

MARTINA.   Look, look!

CLODESUIDA [*covering her eyes*]. It has to be
For our good; we must endure these things, to destroy
Error, and so the gods will warm towards us.

QUICHELM. Here comes my father home!

OSMER.   Well, home he comes.
We're in the right.

TADFRID.   He will understand this tree
By reason of our plight had to bear such fruit.
[*Enter* CYMEN. *He goes towards the barn, near which*
CLODESUIDA *is now standing.*

CYMEN. Clodesuida, a peaceful heart to you now.
I am well; I have seen our terrible gods come down
To beg the crumbs which fall from our sins, their only
Means of life. This evening you and I
Can walk under the trees and be ourselves
Together, knowing that this wild day has gone
For good. Where is the Briton? You still think
You must be afraid and see in him
The seed of a storm. But I have heard

Word of his God, and felt our lonely flesh
Welcome to creation. The fearful silence
Became the silence of great sympathy,
The quiet of God and man in the mutual word.
And never again need we sacrifice, on and on
And on, greedy of the gods' goodwill
But always uncertain; for sacrifice
Can only perfectly be made by God
And sacrifice has so been made, by God
To God in the body of God with man,
On a tree set up at the four crossing roads
Of earth, heaven, time, and eternity
Which meet upon that cross. I have heard this;
And while we listened, with our eyes half-shut
Facing the late sun, above the shoulder
Of the speaking man I saw the cross-road tree,
The love of the God hung on the motes and beams
Of light, as though—

MARTINA.   Father!

                                    [CYMEN *turns and sees* HOEL.

CYMEN.   Is it also here?
Can the sun have written it so hotly on to my eyes—
What have you done?

OSMER.   The unavoidable moment
Came while you were gone—

CYMEN.   What have you done?

TADFRID. Would *you* not break the body of our evil?

CYMEN. I will tell you what I know. Cut him down.
O pain of the world!—I will tell you what I know.
Bring him here to me.

CLODESUIDA.   We have to live.

CYMEN. We have still to learn to live.
> [*They bring* HOEL *to* CYMEN.
>> They say
>
> The sacrifice of God was brought about
> By the blind anger of men, and yet God made
> Their blindness their own saving and lonely flesh
> Welcome to creation. Briton, boy,
> Your God is here, waiting in this land again.
> Forgive me for the sorrow of this world.

MARTINA. You haven't made the sorrow—

CYMEN. All make all:
> For while I leave one muscle of my strength
> Undisturbed, or hug one coin of ease
> Or private peace while the huge debt of pain
> Mounts over all the earth,
> Or, fearing for myself, take half a stride
> Where I could leap; while any hour remains
> Indifferent, I have no right or reason
> To raise a cry against this blundering cruelty
> Of man.

OSMER. Shall we let the light of our lives
> Be choked by darkness?

CYMEN. Osmer,
> What shall we do? We are afraid
> To live by rule of God, which is forgiveness,
> Mercy, and compassion, fearing that by these
> We shall be ended. And yet if we could bear
> These three through dread and terror and terror's doubt,
> Daring to return good for evil without thought
> Of what will come, I cannot think
> We should be the losers. Do we believe
> There is no strength in good or power in God?

God give us courage to exist in God,
And lonely flesh be welcome to creation.
Carry him in.
> [*As they carry* HOEL *away*, CYMEN, CLODESUIDA, *and*
> MARTINA *following, the voices of Augustine's men are heard
> singing.*

THE END

THE LADY'S NOT FOR BURNING

A Comedy

SECOND EDITION

with revisions made for the Candida Plays production, 1971
directed by the author, and the
Chichester Festival Theatre production, 1972
directed by Robin Phillips

To
ALEC CLUNES

THE LADY'S NOT FOR BURNING

Arts Theatre, London: 10 *March* 1948

Richard . . .	DEREK BLOMFIELD
Thomas Mendip .	ALEC CLUNES
Alizon Eliot .	DAPHNE SLATER
Nicholas Devize .	MICHAEL GOUGH
Margaret Devize .	HENZIE RAEBURN
Humphrey Devize .	GORDON WHITING
Hebble Tyson . .	ANDREW LEIGH.
Jennet Jourdemayne .	SHEILA MANAHAN
The Chaplain . .	FRANK NAPIER
Edward Tappercoom .	PETER BULL
Matthew Skipps. .	MORRIS SWEDEN

Directed by Jack Hawkins

Globe Theatre, London: 11 *May* 1949

Richard . . .	RICHARD BURTON
Thomas Mendip .	JOHN GIELGUD
Alizon Eliot .	CLAIRE BLOOM
Nicholas Devize. .	DAVID EVANS
Margaret Devize .	NORA NICHOLSON
Humphrey Devize .	RICHARD LEECH
Hebble Tyson . .	HARCOURT WILLIAMS
Jennet Jourdemayne .	PAMELA BROWN
The Chaplain . .	ELIOT MAKEHAM
Edward Tappercoom .	PETER BULL
Matthew Skipps. .	ESME PERCY

Directed by John Gielgud *and* Esme Percy

Scenery and costumes by Oliver Messel

CHARACTERS

(in order of their appearance)

RICHARD, *an orphaned clerk*

THOMAS MENDIP, *a discharged soldier*

ALIZON ELIOT

NICHOLAS DEVIZE

MARGARET DEVIZE, *mother of Nicholas*

HUMPHREY DEVIZE, *brother of Nicholas*

HEBBLE TYSON, *the Mayor*

JENNET JOURDEMAYNE

THE CHAPLAIN

EDWARD TAPPERCOOM, *a Justice*

MATTHEW SKIPPS

SCENE

A room in the house of Hebble Tyson, Mayor
of the small market-town of Cool Clary

TIME

1400 either more or less or exactly

'In the past I wanted to be hung. It was worth while being hung to be a hero, seeing that life was not really worth living.'

A convict who confessed falsely
to a murder, February 1947

ACT ONE

The Scene (the house of HEBBLE TYSON, *the Mayor of the little market town of Cool Clary) and the appearance of the characters are as much fifteenth century as anything.*

RICHARD, *a young copying-clerk, stands working at a desk.* THOMAS
   MENDIP, *less young, in his late twenties perhaps, and less re-*
   spectable, looks in through a great window from the garden.

THOMAS. Soul!

RICHARD.   —and the plasterer, that's fifteen groats——

THOMAS. Hey, soul!

RICHARD.   —for stopping the draught in the privy——

THOMAS.   Body!
   You calculating piece of clay!

RICHARD.   Damnation.

THOMAS.   Don't mention it. I've never seen a world
   So festering with damnation. I have left
   Rings of beer on every alehouse table
   From the salt sea-coast across half a dozen counties,
   But each time I thought I was on the way
   To a faintly festive hiccup
   The sight of the damned world sobered me up again.
   Where is the Mayor? I've business with His Worship.

RICHARD. Where have you come from?

THOMAS.   Straight from your
   local.
   Damnation's pretty active there this afternoon,
   Licking her lips over gossip of murder and witchcraft;
   There's mischief brewing for someone. Where's the Mayor?

RICHARD.   I'm the mayor's clerk.

THOMAS.   How are you?

RICHARD. Can I have your name?

THOMAS.   It's yours.

RICHARD.   Now, look——

THOMAS.   It's no earthly
Use to me. I travel light; as light,
That is, as a man can travel who will
Still carry his body around because
Of its sentimental value. Flesh
Weighs like a thousand years, and every morning
Wakes heavier for an intake of uproariously
Comical dreams which smell of henbane.
Guts, humours, ventricles, nerves, fibres
And fat—the arterial labyrinth, body's hell.
Still, it was the first thing my mother gave me,
God rest her soul. What were you saying?

RICHARD.   Name
And business.

THOMAS.   Thomas Mendip. My well-born father,
If birth can ever be said to be well, maintains
A castle as draughty as a tree. At every sunset,
It falls into the river and fish swim through its walls.
They swim into the bosom of my grandmother
Who sits late, watching for the constellation of Orion
Because my dead grandfather, she believes,
Is situated somewhere in the Belt.
That is part of the glory of my childhood.

RICHARD. I like you as much as I've liked anybody.
Perhaps you're a little drunk. But here, I'm afraid,
They may not take to you.

THOMAS.   That's what I hope.

RICHARD. Who told you to come here?
You couldn't have chosen a less fortunate afternoon.
They're expecting company—well, a girl. Excuse me,
I must get back to the books.

THOMAS.   I'll wait.

RICHARD.   He'll not
See anybody; I'm sure of it.

THOMAS.   Dear boy,
I only want to be hanged. What possible
Objection can he have to that?

RICHARD.   Why, no, I—
To be—*want* to be hanged? How very drunk you are
After all. Who ever would want to be hanged?

THOMAS.   You don't
Make any allowance for individuality.
How do you know that out there, in the day or night
According to latitude, the entire world
Isn't wanting to be hanged? Now you, for instance,
Still damp from your cocoon, you're desperate
To fly into any noose of the sun that should dangle
Down from the sky. Life, forbye, is the way
We fatten for the Michaelmas of our own particular
Gallows. What a wonderful thing is metaphor.

RICHARD. Was that a knock?

THOMAS.   The girl. She knocks. I saw her
Walking through the garden beside a substantial nun.
Whsst! Revelation!

    Enter ALIZON ELIOT, *aged seventeen, talking to herself.*

ALIZON. Two steps down, she said. One, two,
  The floor. Now I begin to be altogether
  Different—I suppose.

RICHARD.   O God, God,
  God, God, God. I can see such trouble!
  Is life sending a flame to nest in my flax?
  For pity's sake!

THOMAS.   Sweet pretty noose, nice noose.

RICHARD. Will you step in?

ALIZON.   They told me no one was here.

RICHARD. It would be me they meant.

ALIZON.   Oh, would it be?
  Coming in from the light, I am all out at the eyes.
  Such white doves were paddling in the sunshine
  And the trees were as bright as a shower of broken glass.
  Out there, in the sparkling air, the sun and the rain
  Clash together like the cymbals clashing
  When David did his dance. I've an April blindness.
  You're hidden in a cloud of crimson catherine-wheels.

RICHARD. It doesn't really matter. Sit in the shadow.

THOMAS. There are plenty to choose from.

ALIZON.   Oh, there are three of us!
  Forgive me.

RICHARD.   He's waiting—he wants—he says——

THOMAS.   I breathe,
  I spit, I am. But take no further notice.
  I'll just nod in at the window like a rose;
  I'm a black and frosted rosebud whom the good God
  Has preserved since last October. Take no notice.

ALIZON. Men, to me, are a world to themselves.

RICHARD.   Do you think so?

ALIZON. I am going to be married to one of them, almost at once.
I have met him already.

RICHARD.   Humphrey.

ALIZON.   Are you his brother?

RICHARD. No. All I can claim as my flesh and blood
Is what I stand up in. I wasn't born,
I was come-across. In the dusk of one Septuagesima
A priest found an infant, about ten inches long,
Crammed into the poor-box. The money had all
Been taken. Nothing was there except myself,
I was the baby, as it turned out. The priest,
Thinking I might have eaten the money, held me
Upside down and shook me, which encouraged me
To live, I suppose, and I lived.

ALIZON.   No father or mother?

RICHARD. Not noticeably.

ALIZON.   You mustn't let it make you
Conceited. Pride is one of the deadly sins.

THOMAS. And it's better to go for the lively ones.

ALIZON.   Which ones
Do you mean?

THOMAS.   Pay no heed. I was nodding in.

ALIZON. I am quite usual, with five elder sisters. My birth
Was a great surprise to my parents, I think. There had been
A misunderstanding and I appeared overnight
As mushrooms do. My father thought
He would never be able to find enough husbands

For six of us, and so he made up his mind
To simplify matters and let me marry God.
He gave me to a convent.

RICHARD. What showing did he think he would make as God's
Father-in-law?

ALIZON.   He let his beard grow longer.
But he found that husbands fell into my sisters' laps.
So then he stopped thinking of God as eligible—
No prospects, he thought. And so he looked round and found me
Humphrey Devize. Do you think he will do?

RICHARD.   Maybe.
He isn't God, of course.

ALIZON.   No, he isn't.
He's very nearly black.

RICHARD.   Swart.

ALIZON.   Is that it?
When he dies it may be hard to picture him
Agreeable to the utter white of heaven.
Now you, you are——

RICHARD.   Purgatory-colour.

ALIZON. It's on the way to grace. Who are you?

RICHARD.   Richard,
The mayor's copying-clerk.

ALIZON.   The mayor is Humphrey's
Uncle. Humphrey's mother is the mayor's sister.
And then, again, there's Nicholas, Humphrey's brother.
Is he sensible?

RICHARD.   He knows his way about.

THOMAS. O enviable Nick.

RICHARD.   He's nodding in.

ALIZON. I'll tell you a strange thing. Humphrey Devize
   Came to the convent to see me, bringing a present
   For his almost immediate wife, he said, which is me,
   Of barley-sugar and a cross of seed-pearls. Next day
   Nicholas came, with a little cold pie, to say
   He had a message from Humphrey. And then he sat
   And stared and said nothing until he got up to go.
   I asked him for the message, but by then
   It had gone out of his head. Quite gone, you see.
   It was curious.—Now you're not speaking either.

RICHARD. Yes, of course; of course it was curious.

ALIZON. Men are strange. It's almost unexpected
   To find they speak English. Do you think so too?

RICHARD. Things happen to them.

ALIZON.   What things?

RICHARD.   Machinations of nature;
   As April does to the earth.

ALIZON.   I wish it were true!
   Show me daffodils happening to a man!

RICHARD. Very easily.

THOMAS.   And thistles as well, and ladies'
   Bedstraw and deadly nightshade and the need
   For rhubarb.

ALIZON.   Is it a riddle?

RICHARD.   Very likely.
   Certainly a considerable complication.

            Enter NICHOLAS DEVIZE, *muddy, dishevelled.*

NICHOLAS. Where are you, Alizon? Alizon, what do you think?
   I've won you from him! I've destroyed my brother!

                                                E

It's me you're going to marry. What do you think
Of that?

RICHARD. You have mud in your mouth.

NICHOLAS.   You canter off.

ALIZON. No, Nicholas. That's untrue. I have to be
The wife of Humphrey.

NICHOLAS.   Heaven says no. Heaven
And all the nodding angels say
Alizon for Nicholas, Nicholas for Alizon.
You must come to know me; not so much now, because now
I'm excited, but I have at least three virtues.
How many have you got?

RICHARD.   Are you mad? Why don't you
Go and clean yourself up?

NICHOLAS.   What shall I do
With this nattering wheygoose, Alizon?
Shall I knock him down?

ALIZON.   His name is Richard, he says;
And I think he might knock you down.

THOMAS.   Nicholas,
He might. There you have a might, for once,
That's right. Forgive me; an unwarranted interruption.

NICHOLAS. Come in, come in.—Alizon, dear, this Richard
Is all very well. But I was conceived the night
The church was struck by lightning
And born in the great gale. I apologize
For boasting, but once you know my qualities
I can drop back into a quite brilliant

Humility. God have mercy upon me,
You have such little hands. I knew I should love you.

RICHARD. Just tell me: am I to knock him down? You have only
To say so.

ALIZON.　　No, oh no. We only have
To be patient and unweave him. He is mixed,
Aren't you, Nicholas?

NICHOLAS.　　　　Compounded of explosives
Like the world's inside. I'm the receipt God followed
In the creation. It took the roof off his oven.
How long will it be before you love me, Alizon?
Let's go.

[*He picks her up in his arms.*

Enter MARGARET DEVIZE.

MARGARET. Where are you taking Alizon, Nicholas?

NICHOLAS. Out into the air, mother.

MARGARET.　　　　Unnecessary.
She's in the air already. This room is full of it.
Put her down, Nicholas. You look
As though you had come straight out of a wheelbarrow;
And not even straight out.

NICHOLAS.　　　　I have to tell you
I've just been reborn.

MARGARET.　　　Nicholas, you always think
You can do things better than your mother. You can be sure
You were born quite adequately on the first occasion.
There is someone here I don't know. Who is it, Alizon?
Did he come with you?

ALIZON.　　　　Oh, no. A rosebud, he says,
He budded in October.

MARGARET. He's not speaking the truth.—Tch! more rain!
This is properly April.—And you're eager to see
Your handsome Humphrey. Nicholas will fetch him.
They're inseparable, really twin natures, utterly
Brothers, like the two ends of the same thought.—
Nicholas, dear, call Humphrey.

NICHOLAS.   I can't. I've killed him

MARGARET. Fetch Humphrey, Nicholas dear.

NICHOLAS.   I've killed him, dearest
Mother.

MARGARET. Well, never mind. Call Humphrey, dear.

THOMAS. Is that the other end of this happy thought,
There, prone in the flower-bed?

RICHARD.   Yes, it's Humphrey
Lying in the rain.

MARGARET.   One day I shall burst my bud
Of calm, and blossom into hysteria.
Tell him to get up. What on earth is he doing
Lying in the rain?

THOMAS.   All flesh is grass.

ALIZON. Have you really killed Humphrey?

MARGARET.   Nicholas,
Your smile is no pleasure to me.

NICHOLAS.   We fought for possession
Of Alizon Eliot. What could be more natural?
What he loves, I love. And if existence will
Disturb a man with beauty, how can he help
Trying to impose on her the boundary

Of his two bare arms?—Pandemonium, what a fight!
What a fight! Humphrey went hurtling
Like Lucifer into the daffodils.
When Babylon fell there wasn't a better thump.

MARGARET. Are you standing there letting your brother be rained
　　on?
Haven't you any love for him?

NICHOLAS.　　　　　　　　　Yes, mother,
But wet as well as dry.

MARGARET.　　　　　Can Richard carry him
Single-handed?

NICHOLAS.　　　Why can't he use both hands?
And how did I know it was going to rain?

　　　　　　　　　　　　　　[*Exit* NICHOLAS *with* RICHARD.

MARGARET. I would rather have to plait the tails of unbroken
Ponies than try to understand Nicholas.
Oh! it's bell-ringing practice. Their ding-dong rocks me
Till my head feels like the belfry, and makes blisters
All along my nerves. Dear God, a cuckoo
As well!

THOMAS. By God, a cuckoo! Grief and God,
A canting cuckoo, that laugh with no smile!
A world unable to die sits on and on
In spring sunlight, hatching egg after egg,
Hoping against hope that out of one of them
Will come the reason for it all; and always
Out pops the arid chuckle and centuries
Of cuckoo-spit.

MARGARET.　　　　I don't really think we need
To let that worry us now. I don't know why you're waiting,

Or who brought you, or whether I could even
Begin to like you, but I know it would be agreeable
If you left us. There's enough going on already.

THOMAS. There is certainly enough going on.
 Madam, watch Hell come
As a gleam into the eye of the wholesome cat
When philip-sparrow flips his wing.
I see a gleam of Hell in *you*, madam.
You understand those bells perfectly.
I understand them, too.
What is it that, out there in the mellow street,
The soft rain is raining on?
Is it only on the little sour grass, madam?

MARGARET. Out in the street? What could it be?

THOMAS.   It could be,
 And it is, a witch-hunt.

MARGARET.   Oh!—dear; another?

THOMAS. Your innocence is on at such a rakish angle
It gives you quite an air of iniquity.
Hadn't you better answer that bell? With a mere
Clouding of your unoccupied eyes, madam,
Or a twitch of the neck: what better use can we put
Our faces to than to have them express kindness
While we're thinking of something else? Oh, be disturbed,
Be disturbed, madam, to the extent of a tut
And I will thank God for civilization.
This is my last throw, my last poor gamble
On the human heart.

MARGARET.   If I knew who you were
 I should ask you to sit down. But while you're on

Your feet, would you be kind enough to see
How Humphrey is doing?

THOMAS.   If we listened, we could hear
How the hunters, having washed the dinner things,
Are now toiling up and down the blind alleys
Which they think are their immortal souls,
To scour themselves in the blood of a grandmother.
They, of course, will feel all the better for it.
But she? Grandma? Is it possible
She may be wishing she had died yesterday,
The wicked sobbing old body of a woman?·

MARGARET. At the moment, as you know,
I'm trying hard to be patient with my sons.
You really mustn't expect me to be Christian
In two directions at once.

THOMAS.   What, after all,
Is a halo? It's only one more thing to keep clean.
Richard and Nicholas
Have been trying to persuade the body to stand up.

ALIZON. Why, yes, he isn't dead. He's lying on his back
Picking the daffodils. And now they are trying
To lift him.

MARGARET.   Let me look over your shoulder.
They mustn't see me taking an interest.
Oh, the poor boy looks like a shock
Of bedraggled oats.—But you will see, Alizon,
What a nice boy he can be when he wears a clean shirt.
I more than once lost my heart to clean linen
When I was a young creature, even to linen
That hung on the hedges without a man inside it.
Do I seem composed, sufficiently placid and unmotherly?

ALIZON. Altogether, except that your ear-ring
Trembles a little.

MARGARET.   It's always our touches of vanity
That manage to betray us.

THOMAS.   When shall I see the mayor?
I've had enough of the horror beating in the belfry.
Where is the mayor?

Re-enter RICHARD *and* NICHOLAS *carrying* HUMPHREY *who has a
bunch of daffodils in his hand.*

NICHOLAS.   Here's Humphrey. Where would you like him?

MARGARET. Humphrey, why do you have to be carried?

HUMPHREY.   My dear
Mother, I didn't knock myself down. Why
Should I pick myself up?—Daffodils
For my future wife.

NICHOLAS.   You swindling half-cock alderman!
Do I have to kill you a second time?
I've proved my right to have her.

HUMPHREY. Nothing of the sort. Officially
Alizon is mine. What is official
Is incontestable.—Without disrespect either
To you, mother, or to my officially
Dear one, I shall lie down.—Who is playing the viol?

MARGARET. The Chaplain is tuning his G string by the bells.
It must be time for prayers. It must be time
For something. You're both transfigured with dirt.

THOMAS. Where in thunder is the mayor? Are you deaf to the
baying

Of those human bloodhounds out in the street?
I want to be hanged.

NICHOLAS [*to* HUMPHREY]. You dismal coprolite!
It's in my stars I should have her. Wait
Till it's dark, and go out if you dare
Bareheaded under the flash of my star Mercury.
Ignore the universe if you can. Go on,
Ignore it!—Alizon, who's going to marry you?

MARGARET. He deserves no answer.

RICHARD.   Can you tell us, Alizon?

ALIZON. I am not very used to things happening rapidly.
The nuns, you see, were very quiet, especially
In the afternoon. They say I shall marry Humphrey.

MARGARET. Certainly so. Now, Nicholas, go and get clean.

NICHOLAS. She never shall!

THOMAS.   Will someone fetch the mayor?
Will no one make the least effort to let me
Out of the world?

NICHOLAS.   Let Humphrey go and officially
Bury himself. She's not for him.
What does love understand about hereinafter-
Called-the-bride-contracted?
An April anarchy, she is, with a dragon's breath,
An angel on a tiger,
The jaws and maw of a kind of heaven, though hell
Sleeps there with one open eye; an onslaught
Unpredictable made by a benefactor
Armed to the teeth——

THOMAS.   Who benefits, before God,

By this collision of the sexes,
This paroxysm of the flesh? Let me get out!
I'll find the mayor myself
And let you go on with your psalm of love.

                        [He makes for the door.

HUMPHREY. Who the hell's that?

RICHARD.   The man about the gallows.

    Enter HEBBLE TYSON *the mayor, afflicted with office.*

MARGARET. Now here's your uncle. Do, for the sake of calm,
Go and sweeten yourselves.

THOMAS.   Is this the man
I long for?

TYSON.   Pest, who has stolen my handkerchief?

MARGARET. Use this one, Hebble.—Go and get under the pump.

                    [Exit HUMPHREY *and* NICHOLAS.

TYSON [*blowing his nose*]. Noses, noses.

THOMAS.   Mr. Mayor, it's a joy to see you.
You're about to become my gateway to eternal
Rest.

TYSON.   Dear sir, I haven't yet been notified
Of your existence. As far as I'm concerned
You don't exist. Therefore you are not entitled
To any rest at all, eternal or temporary,
And I would be obliged if you'd sit down.

MARGARET. Here is Alizon Eliot, Humphrey's bride
To be.

THOMAS. I have come to be hanged, do you hear?

TYSON. Have you filled in the necessary forms?—

So this is the young lady? Very nice, very charming.—
And a very pretty dress.
Splendid material, a florin a yard
If a groat. I'm only sorry you had to come
On a troubled evening such as this promises
To be. The bells, you know. Richard, my boy,
What is it this importunate fellow wants?

RICHARD. He says he wants to be hanged, sir.

TYSON.   Out of the question
It's a most immodest suggestion, which I know
Of no precedent for. Cannot be entertained.
I suspect an element of mockery
Directed at the ordinary decencies
Of life.—Tiresome catarrh.—A sense of humour
Incompatible with good citizenship
And I wish you a good evening. Are we all
Assembled together for evening prayers?

THOMAS.   Oh no!
You can't postpone me. Since opening-time I've been
Propped up at the bar of heaven and earth, between
The wall-eye of the moon and the brandy-cask of the sun,
Growling thick songs about jolly good fellows
In a mumping pub where the ceiling drips humanity,
Until I've drunk myself sick, and now, by Christ,
I mean to sleep it off in a stupor of dust
Till the morning after the day of judgement.
So put me on the waiting-list for your gallows
With a note recommending preferential treatment.

TYSON. Go away; you're an unappetizing young man
With a tongue too big for your brains. I'm not at all sure
It would be amiss to suppose you to be a vagrant,

In which case an unfortunate experience
At the cart's tail——

THOMAS.   Unacceptable.
Hanging or nothing.

TYSON.   Get this man away from here!
Good gracious, do you imagine the gallows to be
A charitable institution? Very mad,
Wishes to draw attention to himself;
The brain a delicate mechanism; Almighty
God more precise than a clockmaker;
Grant us all a steady pendulum.

ALL. Amen.

THOMAS. Listen! The wild music of the spheres:
Tick-tock.

RICHARD.   Come on; you've got to go.

THOMAS. Does Justice with her sweet, impartial sword
Never come to this place? Do you mean
There's no recognition given to murder here?

MARGARET. Murder?

TYSON.   Now what is it?

THOMAS.   I'm not a fool.
I didn't suppose you would do me a favour for nothing.
No crime, no hanging; I quite understand the rules.
But I've made that all right. I managed to do-in
A rag-and-bone merchant at the bottom of Leapfrog Lane.

TYSON [*staring*]. Utterly unhinged.

MARGARET.   Hebble, they're all
In the same April fit of exasperating nonsense.

Nicholas, too. He said he had killed Humphrey
But of course he hadn't. If he had I should have told you.

THOMAS. It was such a monotonous cry, that 'Raga-boa!'
Like the damned cuckoo. It was more than time
He should see something of another world.
But, poor old man, he wasn't anxious to go.
He picked on his rags and his bones as love
Picks upon hearts, he with an eye to profit
And love with an eye to pain.

RICHARD.   *Sanctus fumus!*

TYSON. Get a complete denial of everything
He has said. I don't want to be bothered with you.
You don't belong to this parish. I'm perfectly satisfied
He hasn't killed a man.

THOMAS.   I've killed two men
If you want me to be exact.
The other I thought scarcely worth mentioning:
A quite unprepossessing pig-man with a birthmark.
He couldn't have had any affection for himself.
So I pulped him first and knocked him into the river
Where the water gives those girlish giggles around
The ford, and held him under with my foot
Until he was safely in Abram's bosom, birthmark
And all. You see, it still isn't properly dry.

TYSON. What a confounded thing! Who do people
Think they are, coming here without
Identity, and putting us to considerable
Trouble and expense to have them punished?
You don't deserve to be listened to.

THOMAS.   It's habit.
I've been unidentifiably

Floundering in Flanders for the past seven years,
Prising open ribs to let men go
On the indefinite leave which needs no pass.
And now all roads are uncommonly flat, and all hair
Stands on end.

Enter NICHOLAS.

NICHOLAS.   I'm sorry to interrupt
But there's a witch to see you, uncle.

TYSON.   To see me?
A witch to see me? I will not be the toy
Of irresponsible events. Is that clear
To you all?

NICHOLAS.   Yes. But she's here.

TYSON.   A witch to see me!
Do I have to tell you what to do with her?

NICHOLAS. Don't tell me. My eyes do that only too well.
She is the one, of witches she's the one
Who most of all disturbs Hell's heart. Jimminy!
How she must make Torment sigh
To have her to add to its torment! How the flames
Must burn to lay their tongues about her.
If evil has a soul it's here outside,
The flower of sin, Satan's latest
Button-hole. Shall I ask her in?

THOMAS.   She's young,
O God, she's young.

TYSON.   I stare at you, Nicholas,
With no word of condemnation. I stare,
Astonished at your behaviour.

MARGARET.   Ask her in?
  In here? Nicholas——

NICHOLAS.   She's the glorious
  Undercoat of this painted world——

                    [JENNET JOURDEMAYNE *stands in the doorway.*

                                    ——You see:
  It comes through, however much of our whiteness
  We paint over it.

TYSON.   What is the meaning of this?
  What is the meaning of this?

THOMAS.   That's the most relevant
  Question in the world.

JENNET.   Will someone say
  Come in? And understand that I don't every day
  Break in on the quiet circle of a family
  At prayers? Not quite so unceremoniously,
  Or so shamefully near a flood of tears,
  Or looking as unruly as I surely do. Will you
  Forgive me?

TYSON.   You'll find I can't be disarmed
  With pretty talk, young woman. You have no business
  At all in this house.

JENNET.   Do you know how many walls
  There are between the garden of the Magpie,
  Past Lazer's field, Slink Alley and Poorsoul Pond
  To the gate of your paddock?

TYSON.   I'm not to be seduced.
  I'm not attending.

JENNET.   Eight. I've come over them all.

MARGARET. How could she have done?

THOMAS.   Her broomstick's in the hall.

MARGARET. Come over to this side of the room, Nicholas.

NICHOLAS. Don't worry, mother, I have my fingers crossed.

TYSON. Never before in the whole term of my office
Have I met such extraordinary ignorance
Of what is permitted——

JENNET.   Indeed, I was ignorant.
They were hooting and howling for me, as though echoes
Could kill me. So I started to run. Thank God
I only passed one small girl in a ditch
Telling the beads of her daisy-chain.
And a rumpled idiot-boy who smiled at me.
They say I have turned a man into a dog.

TYSON.   This will all be gone into
At the proper time——

JENNET.   But it isn't a dog at all,
It's a bitch; a rather appealing brindle bitch
With many fleas. Are you a gentleman
Full of ripe, friendly wisdom?

TYSON.   This
Will all be gone into at the proper——

JENNET.   If so
I will sit at your feet. I will sit anyway;
I am tired. Eight walls are enough.

MARGARET.   What do we do?
I can almost feel the rustling-in of some
Kind of enchantment already.

TYSON.   She will have
To be put in charge.

ALIZON.   Oh, must she, must she?

THOMAS. He can see she's a girl of property,
And the property goes to the town if she's a witch;
She couldn't have been more timely.

NICHOLAS.   Curious, crooked
Beauty of the earth. Fascinating.

TYSON [*to* JENNET]. Get up at once, you undisciplined girl. Have
    you never
Heard of law and order?

NICHOLAS.   Won't you use
This chair?

JENNET.   Thank you. Oh, this is the reasonable
World again! I promise not to leave behind me
Any flymarks of black magic, or any familiars
Such as mice or beetles which might preach
Demonology in your skirting-board.
It's unbelievable, the quite fantastic
Tales they tell!

TYSON.   This will be discussed
At the proper time——

THOMAS.   When we have finished talking
About my murders.

MARGARET. Are they both asking to be punished? Has death
Become the fashionable way to live?
Nothing would surprise me in their generation.

JENNET. Asking to be punished? Why, no, I have come
Here to have the protection of your laughter.
They accuse me of such a brainstorm of absurdities
That all my fear dissolves in the humour of it.
If I could perform what they say I *can* perform

I should have got safely away from here
As fast as you bat your eyelid.

TYSON.   Oh, indeed;
Could you indeed?

JENNET.   They say I have only
To crack a twig, and over the springtime weathercocks
Cloudburst, hail and gale, whatever you will,
Come leaping fury-foremost.

TYSON.   The report
May be exaggerated, of course, but where there's smoke. . .

JENNET. They also say that I bring back the past;
For instance, Helen comes,
Brushing the maggots from her eyes,
And, clearing her throat of several thousand years,
She says 'I loved . . .'; but cannot any longer
Remember names. Sad Helen. Or Alexander, wearing
His imperial cobwebs and breastplate of shining worms
Wakens and looks for his glasses, to find the empire
Which he knows he put beside his bed.

TYSON. Whatever you say will be taken down in evidence
Against you; am I making myself clear?

JENNET. They tell one tale, that once, when the moon
Was gibbous and in a high dazed state
Of nimbus love, I shook a jonquil's dew
On to a pearl and let a cricket chirp
Three times, thinking of pale Peter:
And there Titania was, vexed by a cloud
Of pollen, using the sting of a bee to clean
Her nails and singing, as drearily as a gnat,
'Why try to keep clean?'

THOMAS.   'The earth is all of earth'—

So sang the queen:
So the queen sung,
Crumbling her crownet into clods of dung.

JENNET. You heard her, too, Captain? Bravo. Is that
A world you've got there, hidden under your hat?

THOMAS. Bedlam, ma'am, and the battlefield
Uncle Adam died on. He was shot
To bits with the core of an apple
Which some fool of a serpent in the artillery
Had shoved into God's cannon.

TYSON.　　　　　　　　　That's enough!
Terrible frivolity, terrible blasphemy,
Awful unorthodoxy. I can't understand
Anything that is being said. Fetch a constable.
The woman's tongue clearly knows the flavour
Of *spiritu maligno*. The man must be
Drummed out of the town.

THOMAS.　　　　　　　Oh, *must* he be?

RICHARD. Are you certain, sir? The constable? The lady
Was laughing. She laughed at the very idea
Of being a witch, sir.

TYSON.　　　　　　Yes, just it, just it.
Giving us a rigmarole of her dreams:
Probably dreams: but intentionally
Recollected, intentionally consented to,
Intentionally delighted in. And so
As dangerous as the act. Fetch the constable.

NICHOLAS. Sad, how things always are. We get one gulp
Of dubious air from our hellmost origins
And we have to bung up the draught with a constable.
It's a terribly decontaminating life.

TYSON. I'll not have any frivolity.
The town goes in terror.
I have told you, Richard, twice, what to do.
Are you going about it?

RICHARD.   No, sir. Not yet.

TYSON. Did you speak to me? Now be careful how you answer.

JENNET. Can you be serious? I am Jennet Jourdemayne
And I believe in the human mind. Why play with me
And make me afraid of you, as you did for a moment,
I confess it. You can't believe—oh, surely, not
When the centuries of the world are piled so high—
You'll not believe what, in their innocence,
Those old credulous children in the street
Imagine of me?

THOMAS.   Innocence! Dear girl,
Before the world was, innocence
Was beaten by a lion all round the town.
And liked it.

JENNET.   What, does everyone still knuckle
And suckle at the big breast of irrational fears?
Do they really think I charm a sweat from Tagus,
Or lure an Amazonian gnat to fasten
On William Brown and shake him till he rattles?
Can they think and then think like this?

TYSON.   Will be
Gone into at the proper time. Disturbing
The peace. In every way. Have to arrest you.

JENNET. No!

THOMAS.   You bubble-mouthing, fog-blathering,

Chin-chuntering, chap-flapping, liturgical,
Turgidical, base old man! What about my murders?
And what goes round in *your* head,
What funny little murders and fornications
Chatting up and down in three-four time
Afraid to come out? What bliss to sin by proxy
And do penance by way of someone else!
But we'll not talk about you. It will make the outlook
So dark. Neither about this exquisitely
Mad young woman. Nor about this congenital
Generator, your nephew here;
Nor about anyone but me. I'm due
To be hanged. Good Lord, aren't two murders enough
To win me the medals of damnation? Must I put
Half a dozen children on a spit
And toast them at the flame that comes out of my mouth?
You let the fairies fox you while the devil
Does you. Concentrate on me.

TYSON.   I'll not
Have it—I'll—I'll——

THOMAS.   Power of Job!
Must I wait for a stammer? Your life, sir, is propelled
By a dream of the fear of having nightmares; your love
Is the fear of being alone; your world's history
The fear of a possible leap by a possible antagonist
Out of a possible shadow, or a not-improbable
Skeleton out of your dead-certain cupboard.
But here am I, the true phenomenon
Of acknowledged guilt, steaming with the blood
Of the pig-man and the rag-and-bone man, Crime
Transparent. What the hell are we waiting for?

TYSON. Will you attend to me? Will you be silent?

JENNET. Are you doing this to save me?

THOMAS.   You flatter my powers,
My sweet; you're too much a woman. But if you wish
You can go down to the dinner of damnation
On my arm.

JENNET.   I dine elsewhere.

TYSON.   Am I invisible?
Am I inaudible? Do I merely festoon
The room with my presence? Richard, wretched boy,
If you don't wish to incur considerable punishment
Do yourself the kindness to fetch the constable.
I don't care for these unexpurgated persons.
I shall lose my patience.

MARGARET.   I shall lose my faith
In the good-breeding of providence. Wouldn't this happen
Now: to-day: within an hour or two
Of everyone coming to congratulate
Humphrey and Alizon. Arrangements were made
A month ago, long before this gentleman's
Murders were even thought of.

TYSON.   They don't exist,
I say——

Enter HUMPHREY.

HUMPHREY. Uncle, there's a sizeable rumpus,
Without exaggeration a how-do-you-do
Taking place in the street. I thought you should know.

TYSON. Rumpus?

HUMPHREY.   Perhaps rumpus isn't the word.
A minor kind of bloody revolution.
It's this damned rascal, this half-pay half-wit.

I should say he's certifiable. It seems
He's been spreading all around the town some tale
About drowning a pig-man and murdering old Skipps
The rag-and-bone man.

THOMAS.   Ah, old Skipps, old Skipps,
  What a surplus of bones you'll have where you've gone to now!

JENNET. Old Skipps? But he's the man——

TYSON.   Will you both be silent?
  I won't have every Tom, Dick, and Harry
  Laying information against himself before
  He's got written authority from me.

HUMPHREY.   Quite right.
  As it is, the town is hell's delight. They've looked
  For the drowned pig-man and they've looked for Skipps
  And they've looked in the places where he says he left them
  And they can't find either.

NICHOLAS.   Can't find either?

HUMPHREY. Can't find either.

MARGARET.   Of course they can't. When he first
  Mentioned murders I knew he had got hold
  Of a quite wrong end of the stick.

HUMPHREY.   They say he's the Devil.

MARGARET. I can imagine who started *that* story.

HUMPHREY. But are we so sure he isn't? Outside in the street
  They're convinced he's the Devil. And none of us ever having
  Seen the Devil, how can we know? They say
  He killed the old men and spirited them into the Limbo.
  We can't search there. I don't even know where it is.

THOMAS. Sir, it's between me and the deep blue sea.
The wind of conscience blows straight from its plains.

HUMPHREY. Shut up.—If you're the Devil I beg your pardon.—
They also have the idea
He's got a girl in his toils, a witch called——

JENNET.   Jennet.
I am she.

HUMPHREY. God.

TYSON.   Well, Humphrey, well?
Is that the end of your information?

NICHOLAS.   Humphrey,
Have you spoken to your little future wife
Lately?

THOMAS. Tinder, easy tinder.

HUMPHREY.   In fact—
In fact——

NICHOLAS.   In fact it's all a bloody revolution.

TYSON. I'm being played with, I'm sure of it; something tells me
There is irresponsibility somewhere. Richard,
You'll not get out of this lightly. Where's the constable?
Why isn't he standing before me?

RICHARD.   I can see
No need for the constable, sir.

TYSON.   No need? No need?

Enter the CHAPLAIN *with his viol.*

CHAPLAIN. I am late for prayers, I know; I know you think me
A broken reed, and my instrument too, my better half,
You lacked it, I'm afraid. But life has such
Diversity, I sometimes remarkably lose

Eternity in the passing moment. Just now
In the street there's a certain boisterous interest
In a spiritual matter. They say——

TYSON. I know what they say.

CHAPLAIN. Ah yes; you know. Sin, as well as God,
Moves in a most mysterious way. It is hard to imagine
Why the poor girl should turn Skipps into a dog.

NICHOLAS. Skipps? Skipps into a dog?

HUMPHREY. But Skipps——

THOMAS. Skipps trundles in another place, calling
His raga-boa in gutters without end,
Transfigured by the spatial light
Of Garbage Indestructible. And I
Ought to know since I sent him there. A dog?
Come, come; don't let's be fanciful.

TYSON. They say one thing and another thing and both at once;
I don't know. It will all have to be gone into
At the proper time——

HUMPHREY. But this is a contradiction——

CHAPLAIN. Ah, isn't that life all over? And is this
The young assassin? If he is the doer of the damage
Can it be she also? My flock are employing
Fisticuffs over this very question.

HUMPHREY. But if he could be the Devil——

THOMAS. Good boy! Shall I set
Your minds at rest and give you proof? Come here.

[*He whispers in* HUMPHREY's *ear.*

HUMPHREY. That's not funny.

THOMAS. Not funny for the goats.

HUMPHREY. I've heard it before. He says the Day of Judgement
Is fixed for to-night.

MARGARET.   Oh no. I have always been sure
That when it comes it will come in the autumn.
Heaven, I am quite sure, wouldn't disappoint
The bulbs.

THOMAS.   Consider: vastiness lusted, mother;
A huge heaving desire, overwhelming solitude,
And the mountain belly of Time laboured
And brought forth man, the mouse. The spheres churned on,
Hoping to charm our ears
With sufficient organ-music, sadly sent out
On the wrong wave of sound; but still they roll
Fabulous and fine, a roundabout
Of doomed and golden notes. And on beyond,
Profound with thunder of oceanic power,
Lie the morose dynamics of our dumb friend
Jehovah.
Why should these omnipotent bombinations
Go on with the deadly human anecdote, which
From the first was never more than remotely funny?
No; the time has come for tombs to tip
Their refuse; for the involving ivy, the briar,
The convolutions of convolvulus,
To disentangle and make way
For the last great ascendancy of dust,
Sucked into judgement by a cosmic yawn
Of boredom. The Last Trump
Is timed for twenty-two forty hours precisely.

TYSON. This will all be gone into at the proper——

THOMAS.   Time
   Will soon be most improper. Why not hang me
   Before it's too late?

MARGARET.   I shall go and change my dress;
   Then I shall both be ready for our guests
   And whatever else may come upon the world.

HUMPHREY. I'm sure he's mad.

CHAPLAIN.   And his information, of course,
   Is in opposition to what we are plainly told
   In the Scriptures: that the hour will come——

NICHOLAS.   Do you think
   He means it? I've an idea he's up to something
   None of us knows about, not one of us.

ALIZON [*who has found her way to* RICHARD]. Quiet Richard, son of
   nobody.

RICHARD [*whispering*]. It isn't always like this, I promise it isn't.

JENNET. May I, Jennet Jourdemayne, the daughter
   Of a man who believed the universe was governed
   By certain laws, be allowed to speak?
   Here is such a storm of superstition
   And humbug and curious passions, where will you start
   To look for the truth? Am I in fact
   An enchantress bemused into collaboration
   With the enemy of man? Is this the enemy,
   This eccentric young gentleman never seen by me
   Before? I say I am not. He says perhaps
   He is. You say I am. You say he is not.
   And now the eccentric young gentleman threatens us all
   With imminent cataclysm. If, as a living creature,
   I wish in all good faith to continue living,
   Where do you suggest I should lodge my application?

TYSON. That is perfectly clear. You are both under arrest.

THOMAS. Into Pandora's box with all the ills.
But not if that little hell-cat Hope's
Already in possession. I've hoped enough.
I gave the best years of my life to that girl,
But I'm walking out with Damnation now, and she's
A flame who's got finality.

JENNET. Do you want no hope for me either? No compassion
To lift suspicion off me?

THOMAS.   Lift? Compassion
Has a rupture, lady. To hell with lifting.

JENNET. Listen, please listen to me!

THOMAS.   Let the world
Go, lady; it isn't worth the candle.

TYSON. Take her, Richard; down to the cellars.

THOMAS.   You see?
He has the key to every perplexity.
Kiss your illusions for me before they go.

JENNET. But what will happen?

THOMAS. That's something even old nosedrip doesn't know.

                          [RICHARD *leads* JENNET *away*

TYSON. Take him away!

THOMAS.   Mr. Mayor, hang me for pity's sake,
For God's sake hang me, before I love that woman!

CURTAIN ON ACT ONE

ACT TWO

The same room, about an hour later. The CHAPLAIN *in a chair, sleeping.* TYSON *surrounded with papers.* EDWARD TAPPERCOOM, *the town's Justice, mountainously rolling up and down the room.*

TAPPERCOOM. Well, it's poss-ss-ible, it's poss-ss-ible.
I *may* have been putting the Devil to the torture.
But can you smell scorching?—not a singe
For my sins—that's from yesterday: I leaned
Across a candle. For all practical purposes
I feel as unblasted as on the day I was born.
And God knows I'm a target. Cupid scarcely
Needs to aim, and no devil could miss me.

TYSON. But his action may be delayed. We really must
Feel our way. We don't want to put ourselves wrong
With anything as positive as evil.

TAPPERCOOM. We have put him to the merest thumbscrew,
      Tyson,
Courteously and impartially, the purest
Cajolery to coax him to deny
These cock-and-bull murders for which there isn't a scrap
Of evidence.

TYSON.   Ah; ah. How does he take it?
Has he denied them?

TAPPERCOOM.   On the contrary.
He says he has also committed petty larceny,
Abaction, peculation and incendiarism.
As for the woman Jourdemayne——

151

TYSON.   Ah, yes,
Jourdemayne; what are we to make of her?
Wealthy, they tell me. But on the other hand
Quite affectingly handsome. Sad, you know.
We see where the eye can't come, eh, Tappercoom?
And all's not glorious within; no use
Saying it is.—I had a handkerchief.
Ah yes; buried amongst all this evidence.

TAPPERCOOM. Now, no poetics, Tyson. Blow your nose
And avoid lechery. Keep your eye on the evidence
Against her; there's plenty of it there. Religion
Has made an honest woman of the supernatural
And we won't have it kicking over the traces again,
Will we, Chaplain?—In the Land of Nod.
Admirable man.

TYSON.   Humanity,
That's all, Tappercoom; it's perfectly proper.
No one is going to let it interfere
With anything serious. I use it with great
Discretion, I assure you.—Has she confessed?

TAPPERCOOM. Not at all. Though we administer persuasion
With great patience, she admits nothing. And the man
Won't stop admitting. It really makes one lose
All faith in human nature.

Enter MARGARET, *without her placidity.*

MARGARET.   Who has the tongs?
The tongs, Hebble, the tongs, dear! Sweet
Elijah, we shall all go up in flames!

TYSON. Flames? Did you hear that, Tappercoom? Flames!
My sister said flames!

MARGARET.   A log the size of a cheese
　Has fallen off the fire! Well, where are they?
　What men of action! Tongs, I said!—Chaplain,
　They're under your feet. Very simple you'd look
　As a pile of ashes.

                                                   [Exit.

TYSON.   Oh. I beg your pardon,
　Tappercoom. A blazing log.

CHAPLAIN.   Would there be something
　I could do? I was asleep, you know.

TYSON. All this evidence from the witchfinder. . . .

TAPPERCOOM. The advent of a woman cannot be
　Too gradual. I am not a nervous man
　But I like to be predisposed to an order of events.

CHAPLAIN. It was very interesting: I was dreaming I stood
　On Jacob's ladder, waiting for the Gates to open.
　And the ladder was made entirely of diminished sevenths.
　I was surprised but not put out. Nothing
　Is altogether what we suppose it to be.

TAPPERCOOM. As for the Day of Judgement, we can be sure
　It's not due yet. What are we told the world
　Will be like? 'Boasters, blasphemers, without natural
　Affection, traitors, trucebreakers,' and the rest of it.
　Come, we've still a lot of backsliding ahead of us.

TYSON. Are you uneasy, Tappercoom?

TAPPERCOOM.   No, Tyson.
　The whole thing's a lot of amphigourious
　Stultiloquential fiddle-faddle.

           Re-enter MARGARET, *head-first.*

MARGARET.   Hebble!

TAPPERCOOM. For God's sake!

TYSON.   What is it now? What is it?

MARGARET. The street's gone mad. They've seen a shooting star!

TYSON. They? Who? What of it?

MARGARET.   I'm sure I'm sorry,
But the number of people gone mad in the street
Is particularly excessive. They were shaking
Our gate, and knocking off each other's hats
And six fights simultaneously, and some
Were singing psalm a hundred and forty—I think
It's a hundred and forty—and the rest of them shouting
'The Devil's in there!' (pointing at this house)
'Safety from Satan!' and 'Where's the woman? Where's
The witch? Send her out!'; and using words
That are only fit for the Bible. And I'm sure
There was blood in the gutter from somebody's head
Or else it was the sunset in a puddle,
But Jobby Pinnock was prising up cobblestones,
Roaring like the north wind, and you know
What he is in church when he starts on the responses.
And that old Habbakuk Brown using our wall
As it was never meant to be used. And then
They saw the star fall over our roof somewhere
And followed its course with a downrush of whistling
And Ohs and Ahs and groans and screams; and Jobby
Pinnock dropped a stone on his own foot
And roared 'Almighty God, it's a sign!' and some
Went down on their knees and others fell over them
And they've started to fight again, and the hundred and fortieth
Psalm has begun again louder and faster than ever.
Hebble dear, isn't it time they went home?

TYSON. All right, yes, all right, all right. Now why
Can't people mind their own business? This shooting star
Has got nothing to do with us, I am quite happy
In my mind about that. It probably went past
Perfectly preoccupied with some astral anxiety or other
Without giving us a second thought. Eh, Tappercoom?
One of those quaint astrological holus-boluses,
Quite all right.

TAPPERCOOM. Quite. An excess of phlegm
In the solar system. It was on its way
To a heavenly spittoon. How is that,
How is that? On its way——

TYSON. I consider it unwise
To tempt providence with humour, Tappercoom.

MARGARET. And on the one evening when we expect company!
What company is going to venture to get here
Through all that heathen hullabaloo in the road?
Except the glorious company of the Apostles,
And we haven't enough glasses for all that number.

TAPPERCOOM. Doomsday or not, we must keep our integrity.
We cannot set up dangerous precedents
Of speed. We shall sincerely hope, of course,
That Doomsday will refrain from precipitous action;
But the way we have gone must be the way we arrive.

CHAPLAIN. I wish I were a thinking man, very much.
Of course I feel a good deal, but that's no help to you.

TYSON. I'm not bewildered, I assure you I'm not
Bewildered. As a matter of fact a plan
Is almost certainly forming itself in my head
At this very moment. It may even be adequate.

F

CHAPLAIN. Where did I put my better half? I laid it
  Aside. I could take it down to the gate and perhaps
  Disperse them with a skirmish or two of the bow.
  Orpheus, you know, was very successful in that way,
  But of course I haven't his talent, not nearly his talent.

TYSON. If you would allow me to follow my train of thought——

TAPPERCOOM. It's my belief the woman Jourdemayne
  Got hold of the male prisoner by unlawful
  Supernatural soliciting
  And bewitched him into a confession of murder
  To draw attention away from herself. But the more
  We coax him to withdraw his confession, the more
  Crimes he confesses to.

CHAPLAIN.   I know I am not
  A practical person; legal matters and so forth
  Are Greek to me, except, of course,
  That I understand Greek. And what may seem nonsensical
  To men of affairs like yourselves might not seem so
  To me, since everything astonishes me,
  Myself most of all. When I think of myself
  I can scarcely believe my senses. But there it is,
  All my friends tell me I actually exist
  And by an act of faith I have come to believe them.
  But this fellow who is being such a trouble to us,
  He, on the contrary, is so convinced
  He *is* that he wishes he was NOT. Now why
  Should that be?

TAPPERCOOM.   I believe you mean to tell us,
  Chaplain.

MARGARET. I might as well sit down, for all
  The good that standing up does.

CHAPLAIN.   I imagine
  He finds the world not entirely salubrious.
  If he cannot be stayed with flagons, or comforted
  With apples—I quote, of course—or the light, the ocean,
  The ever-changing . . . I mean and stars, extraordinary
  How many, or some instrument or other—I am afraid
  I appear rhapsodical—but perhaps the addition
  Of your thumbscrew will not succeed either. The point
  I'm attempting to make is this one: he might be wooed
  From his aptitude for death by being happier;
  And what I was going to suggest, quite irresponsibly,
  Is that he might be invited to partake
  Of our festivities this evening. No,
  I see it astonishes you.

MARGARET.   Do you mean ask him——

TYSON. I have heard very little of what you have said, Chaplain,
  Being concerned, as I am, with a certain Thought,
  But am I to believe that you recommend our inviting
  This undesirable character to rub shoulders
  With my sister?

CHAPLAIN.   Ah; rubbing shoulders. I hadn't exactly
  Anticipated that. It was really in relation to the soul
  That the possibility crossed my mind——

TAPPERCOOM. As a criminal the boy is a liability.
  I doubt very much if he could supply a farthing
  Towards the cost of his execution. So
  You suggest, Chaplain, we let him bibulate
  From glass to glass this evening, help him to
  A denial of his guilt and get him off our hands
  Before daybreak gets the town on its feet again?

MARGARET. I wish I could like the look of the immediate
  Future, but I don't.

TYSON.   I'm glad to tell you
An idea has formed in my mind, a possible solution.

Enter RICHARD.

RICHARD. Sir, if you please——

TYSON.   Well, Richard?

RICHARD.   I should like to admit
That I've drunk some of the wine put out for the guests.

TYSON. Well, that's a pretty thing, I must say.

RICHARD.   I was feeling
Low; abominably; about the prisoners,
And the row in the street that's getting out of hand—
And certain inner things. And I saw the wine
And I thought Well, here goes, and I drank
Three glassesful.

TYSON.   I trust you feel better for it.

RICHARD. I feel much worse. Those two, sir, the prisoners,
What are you doing with them? I don't know why
I keep calling you Sir. I'm not feeling respectful.
If only inflicted pain could be as contagious
As a plague, you might use it more sparingly.

TAPPERCOOM. Who's this cub of a boy?

MARGARET.   Richard, be sensible.
He's a dear boy but a green boy, and I'm sure
He'll apologize in a minute or two.

TYSON.   The boy
Is a silly boy, he's a silly boy; and I'm going
To punish him.

MARGARET.   Where are Humphrey and Nicholas?

TYSON. Now, Margaret——

RICHARD.   They were where the prisoners are,
Down in the cellars.

MARGARET.   Not talking to that witch?

RICHARD. There isn't a witch. They were sitting about on barrels.
It seemed that neither would speak while the other was there
And neither would go away. Half an hour ago.
They may be there still.

TYSON.   I must remind you, Margaret,
I was speaking to this very stupid boy.
He is going to scrub the floor. Yes, scrub it.
Scrub this floor this evening before our guests
Put in an appearance. Mulish tasks for a mulish
Fellow. I haven't forgotten his refusal
To fetch the constable.

RICHARD.   Has Alizon Eliot
Been left sitting alone?

MARGARET.   Alizon Eliot
Is not for you to be concerned with, Richard.

TYSON. Am I supposed to be merely exercising my tongue
Or am I being listened to? Do you hear me?

RICHARD. Yes; scrub the floor.—No, she is not;
I know that.

TYSON.   Furthermore, you'll relegate
Yourself to the kitchen to-night, fetching and carrying.
If you wish to be a mule you shall be a mule.
                              [*He hands* RICHARD *a note.*
And take this to whatever splendid fellow's
On duty. You will return with the prisoners
And tell them to remain in this room till I send for them.

—Tactics, Tappercoom: the idea that came to me.
You'll think it very good.—You may go, Richard.

[*Exit* RICHARD.

TAPPERCOOM. I am nothing but the Justice here, of course,
But, perhaps, even allowing for that, you could tell me
What the devil you're up to.

Enter NICHOLAS *with a gash on his forehead, followed more slowly
by* HUMPHREY.

NICHOLAS.   Look, Chaplain: blood.
Fee, fi, fo, fum. Can you smell it?

MARGARET. Now what have you been doing?

NICHOLAS.   Isn't it beautiful?
A splash from the cherry-red river that drives my mill!

CHAPLAIN. Well, yes, it has a cheerful appearance,
But isn't it painful?

MARGARET.   I am sure it's painful.
How did you——

HUMPHREY.   Mother, I make it known publicly:
I'm tired of my little brother. Will you please
Give him to some charity?

NICHOLAS.   Give me to faith
And hope and the revolution of our native town.
I've been hit on the head by two-thirds of a brick.

HUMPHREY. The young fool climbed on the wall and addressed
the crowd.

NICHOLAS. They were getting discouraged. I told them how
happy it made me
To see them interested in world affairs

And how the conquest of evil was being openly
Discussed in this house at that very moment
And then unfortunately I was hit by a brick.

MARGARET. What in the world have world affairs
To do with anything? But we won't argue.

TYSON. I believe that brick to have been divinely delivered,
And richly deserved. And am I to understand
You boys have also attempted conversation
With the prisoners?

HUMPHREY.   Now surely, uncle,
As one of the Town Council I should be allowed
To get a grasp of whatever concerns the welfare
Of the population? Nicholas, I agree,
Had no business on earth to be down there.

NICHOLAS.   I was on
Business of the soul, my sweetheart, business
Of the soul.

MARGARET. You may use that word once too often,
Nicholas. Heaven or someone will take you seriously
And then you *would* look foolish. Come with me
And have your forehead seen to.

NICHOLAS.   But my big brother
Was on business of the flesh, by all the fires
Of Venus, weren't you, Humphrey?

HUMPHREY.   What the hell
Do you mean by that, you little death-watch beetle?

MARGARET. Nicholas, will you come?

NICHOLAS.   Certainly, mother.
                    [*Exit* MARGARET *and* NICHOLAS.

TYSON. How very remarkably insufferable
   Young fellows can sometimes be. One would expect them
   To care to model themselves on riper minds
   Such as our own, Tappercoom. But really
   We might as well have not existed, you know.

TAPPERCOOM. Am I to hear your plan, Tyson, or am I
   Just to look quietly forward to old age?

TYSON. My plan, ah, yes. Conclusive and humane.
   The two are brought together into this room.—
   How does that strike you?

TAPPERCOOM.   It makes a complete sentence:
   Subject: they. Predicate: are brought together——

TYSON. Ah, you will say 'with what object?' I'll tell you. We,
   That is: ourselves, the Chaplain, and my elder nephew—
   Will remain unobserved in the adjoining room
   With the communicating door ajar.—And how
   Does that strike you?

TAPPERCOOM.   With a dull thud, Tyson,
   If I may say so.

TYSON.   I see the idea has eluded you.
   A hypothetical Devil, Tappercoom,
   Brought into conversation with a witch.
   A dialogue of Hell, perhaps, and conclusive.
   Or one or other by their exchange of words
   Will prove to be innocent, or we shall have proof
   Positive of guilt. Does that seem good?

TAPPERCOOM. Good is as good results.

HUMPHREY.   I should never have thought
   You would have done anything so undignified
   As to stoop to keyholes, uncle.

TYSON.   No, no, no.
  The door will be ajar, my boy.

HUMPHREY.   Ah yes,
  That will make us upright.—I can hear them coming.

TYSON [*going*]. Come along, come along.

CHAPLAIN.   'The ears of them that hear
  Shall hearken.' The prophet Isaiah.

TYSON.   Come along, Chaplain.

TAPPERCOOM [*following*]. A drink, Tyson. I wish to slake the
    dryness
  Of my disbelief.

                                    [*They go in. The* CHAPLAIN *returns.*

CHAPLAIN.   I musn't leave my mistress.
  Where are you, angel? Just where chucklehead left her.

                    Enter RICHARD *with* JENNET *and* THOMAS.

RICHARD. He wants you to wait here till he sends for you.
  If in some way—I wish—! I must fetch the scrubbers.

                                            [*Exit* RICHARD.

CHAPLAIN. Ah . . . ah . . . I'm not really here. I came
  For my angel, a foolish way to speak of it,
  This instrument. May I say, a happy issue
  Out of all your afflictions? I hope so.—Well,
  I'm away now.

THOMAS. God bless you, in case you sneeze.

CHAPLAIN. Yes; thank you. I may. And God bless you.

                                            [*Exit* CHAPLAIN.

THOMAS [*at the window*]. You would think by the holy scent of it
    our friend
  Had been baptizing the garden. But it's only
  The heathen rainfall.

JENNET.   Do you think he knows
What has been happening to us?

THOMAS.   Old angel-scraper?
He knows all right. But he's subdued
To the cloth he works in.

JENNET.   How tired I am.

THOMAS. And palingenesis has come again
With a hey and a ho. The indomitable
Perseverance of Persephone
Became ludicrous long ago.

JENNET.   What can you see
Out there?

THOMAS.   Out here? Out here is a sky so gentle
Five stars are ventured on it. I can see
The sky's pale belly glowing and growing big,
Soon to deliver the moon. And I can see
A glittering smear, the snail-trail of the sun
Where it crawled with its golden shell into the hills.
A darkening land sunken into prayer
Lucidly in dewdrops of one syllable,
Nunc dimittis. I see twilight, madam.

JENNET. But what can you hear?

THOMAS.   The howl of human jackals.

Enter RICHARD *with pail and scrubbing-brush.*

RICHARD. Do you mind? I have to scrub the floor.

THOMAS. A good old custom. Always fornicate
Between clean sheets and spit on a well-scrubbed floor.

JENNET. Twilight, double, treble, in and out!
If I try to find my way I bark my brain
On shadows sharp as rocks where half a day
Ago was a soft world, a world of warm

Straw, whispering every now and then
With rats, but possible, possible, not this,
This where I'm lost. The morning came, and left
The sunlight on my step like any normal
Tradesman. But now every spark
Of likelihood has gone. The light draws off
As easily as though no one could die
To-morrow.

THOMAS.   Are you going to be so serious
About such a mean allowance of breath as life is?
We'll suppose ourselves to be caddis-flies
Who live one day. Do we waste the evening
Commiserating with each other about
The unhygienic condition of our worm-cases?
For God's sake, shall we laugh?

JENNET.   For what reason?

THOMAS. For the reason of laughter, since laughter is surely
The surest touch of genius in creation.
Would *you* ever have thought of it, I ask you,
If you had been making man, stuffing him full
Of such hopping greeds and passions that he has
To blow himself to pieces as often as he
Conveniently can manage it—would it also
Have occurred to you to make him burst himself
With such a phenomenon as cachinnation?
That same laughter, madam, is an irrelevancy
Which almost amounts to revelation.

JENNET.   I laughed
Earlier this evening, and where am I now?

THOMAS.   Between
The past and the future which is where you were
Before.

JENNET. Was it for laughter's sake you told them
You were the Devil? Or why did you?

THOMAS.   Honesty,
Madam, common honesty.

JENNET.   Honesty common
With the Devil?

THOMAS.   Gloriously common. It's Evil, for once
Not travelling incognito. It is what it is,
The Great Unspurious.

JENNET.   Thank you for that.
You speak of the world I thought I was waking to
This morning. But horror is walking round me here
Because nothing is as it appears to be.
That's the deep water my childhood had to swim in.
My father was drowned in it.

THOMAS.   He was drowned in what?
In hypocrisy?

JENNET.   In the pursuit of alchemy.
In refusing to accept your dictum 'It is
What it is'. Poor father. In the end he walked
In Science like the densest night. And yet
He was greatly gifted.
When he was born he gave an algebraic
Cry; at one glance measured the cubic content
Of that ivory cone his mother's breast
And multiplied his appetite by five.
So he matured by a progression, gained
Experience by correlation, expanded
Into a marriage by contraction, and by
Certain physical dynamics
Formulated me. And on he went
Still deeper into the calculating twilight

Under the twinkling of five-pointed figures
Till Truth became for him the sum of sums
And Death the long division. My poor father.
What years and powers he wasted.
He thought he could change the matter of the world
From the poles to the simultaneous equator
By strange experiment and by describing
Numerical parabolas.

THOMAS. To change
The matter of the world! Magnificent
Intention. And so he died deluded.

JENNET. As a matter of fact, it wasn't a delusion.
As a matter of fact, after his death
When I was dusting the laboratory
I knocked over a crucible which knocked
Over another which rocked a third, and they poured
And spattered over some copper coins which two days later
By impregnation had turned into solid gold.

THOMAS. Tell that to some sailor on a horse!
If you had such a secret, I
And all my fiendish flock, my incubi,
Succubi, imps and cacodemons, would have leapt
Out of our bath of brimming brimstone, crying
Eureka, cherchez la femme!—Emperors
Would be colonizing you, their mistresses
Patronizing you, ministers of state
Governmentalizing you. And you
Would be eulogized, lionized, probably
Canonized for your divine mishap.

JENNET. But I never had such a secret. It's a secret
Still. What it was I spilt, or to what extent,
Or in what proportion; whether the atmosphere

Was hot, cold, moist or dry, I've never known.
And someone else cán discolour their fingers, tease
Their brains and spoil their eyesight to discover it.
My father broke on the wheel of a dream; he was lost
In a search. And so, for me, the actual!
What I touch, what I see, what I know; the essential fact.

THOMAS. In other words, the bare untruth.

JENNET.   And, if I may say it
Without appearing rude, absolutely
No devils.

THOMAS.   How in the miserable world, in that case,
Do you come to be here, pursued by the local consignment
Of fear and guilt? What possible cause——

JENNET.   Your thumbs.
I'm sure they're giving you pain.

THOMAS.   Listen! by both
My cloven hooves! if you put us to the rack
Of an exchange of sympathy, I'll fell you to the ground.
Answer my question.

JENNET.   Why do they call me a witch?
Remember my father was an alchemist.
I live alone, preferring loneliness
To the companionable suffocation of an aunt.
I still amuse myself with simple experiments
In my father's laboratory. Also I speak
French to my poodle. Then you must know
I have a peacock which on Sundays
Dines with me indoors. Not long ago
A new little serving maid carrying the food
Heard its cry, dropped everything and ran,
Never to come back, and told all whom she met
That the Devil was dining with me.

THOMAS.   It really is
  Beyond the limit of respectable superstition
  To confuse my voice with a peacock's. Don't they know
  I sing solo bass in Hell's Madrigal Club?
  —And as for you, you with no eyes, no ears,
  No senses, you the most superstitious
  Of all—(for what greater superstition
  Is there than the mumbo-jumbo of believing
  In reality?)—you should be swallowed whole by Time
  In the way that you swallow appearances.
  Horns, what a waste of effort it has been
  To give you Creation's vast and exquisite
  Dilemma! where altercation thrums
  In every granule of the Milky Way,
  Persisting still in the dead-sleep of the moon,
  And heckling itself hoarse in that hot-head
  The sun. And as for here, each acorn drops
  Arguing to earth, and pollen's all polemic.—
  We have given you a world as contradictory
  As a female, as cabbalistic as the male,
  A conscienceless hermaphrodite who plays
  Heaven off against hell, hell off against heaven,
  Revolving in the ballroom of the skies
  Glittering with conflict as with diamonds:
  We have wasted paradox and mystery on you
  When all you ask us for, is cause and effect!—
  A copy of your birth-certificate was all you needed
  To make you at peace with Creation. How uneconomical
  The whole thing's been.
JENNET.   This is a fine time
  To scold me for keeping myself to myself and out
  Of the clutch of chaos. I was already
  In a poor way of perplexity and now

You leave me no escape except
Out on a stream of tears.

THOMAS [*falling over* RICHARD *scrubbing*]. Now, none of that!—
Hell!

RICHARD. I beg your pardon.

THOMAS.   Now that I'm down
On my knees I may as well stay here. In the name
Of all who ever were drowned at sea, don't weep!
I never learnt to swim. May God keep you
From being my Hellespont.

JENNET.   What I do
With my own tears is for me to decide.

THOMAS. That's all very well. You get rid of them.
But on whose defenceless head are they going to fall?

JENNET. I had no idea you were so afraid of water.
I'll put them away.

THOMAS.   O Pete, I don't know which
Is worse; to have you crying or to have you behaving
Like Catharine of Aix, who never wept
Until after she had been beheaded, and then
The accumulation of the tears of a long lifetime
Burst from her eyes with such force, they practic'ly winded
Three onlookers and floated the parish priest
Two hundred yards into the entrance-hall
Of a brothel.

JENNET.   Poor Catharine!

THOMAS.   Not at all.
It made her life in retrospect infinitely
More tolerable, and when she got to Purgatory
She was laughing so much they had to give her a sedative.

JENNET. Why should you want to be hanged?

THOMAS.   Madam,
I owe it to myself. But I can leave it
Until the last moment. It will keep
While the light still lasts.

JENNET.   What can we see in this light?
Nothing, I think, except flakes of drifting fear,
The promise of oblivion.

THOMAS.   Nothing can be seen
In the thistle-down, but the rough-head thistle comes.
Rest in that riddle. I can pass to you
Generations of roses in this wrinkled berry.
There: now you hold in your hand a race
Of summer gardens, it lies under centuries
Of petals. What is not, you have in your palm.
Rest in the riddle, rest; why not? This evening
Is a ridiculous wisp of down
Blowing in the air as disconsolately as dust.
And you have your own damnable mystery too,
Which at this moment I could well do without.

JENNET. I know of none. I'm an unhappy fact
Fearing death. This is a strange moment
To feel my life increasing, when this moment
And a little more may be for both of us
The end of time. You've cast your fishing-net
Of eccentricity,
Caught me when I was already lost
And landed me with despairing gills on your own
Strange beach. That's too inhuman of you.

THOMAS.   Inhuman?
If I dared to know what you meant it would sound disastrous!

JENNET. It means I care whether you live or die.

THOMAS. Will you stop frightening me to death?
Do you want our spirits to hobble out of their graves
Enduring twinges of hopeless human affection
As long as death shall last? Still to suffer
Pain in the amputated limb! To feel
Passion *in vacuo*! That is the sort of thing
That causes sun-spots, and the lord knows what
Infirmities in the firmament. I tell you
The heart is worthless,
Nothing more than a pomander's perfume
In the sewerage. And a nosegay of private emotion
Won't distract me from the stench of the plague-pit,
You needn't think it will.—Excuse me, Richard.—
Don't entertain the mildest interest in me
Or you'll have me die screaming.

JENNET.   Why should that be?
If you're afraid of your shadow falling across
Another life, shine less brightly upon yourself,
Step back into the rank and file of men,
Instead of preserving the magnetism of mystery
And your curious passion for death. You are making yourself
A breeding-ground for love and must take the consequences.
But what are you afraid of, since in a little
While neither of us may exist? Either or both
May be altogether transmuted into memory,
And then the heart's obscure indeed.—Richard,
There's a tear rolling out of your eye. What is it?

RICHARD. Oh, that? I don't really know. I have things on my mind.

JENNET. Not us?

RICHARD. Not only.

THOMAS.   If it's a woman, Richard,
  Apply yourself to the scrubbing-brush. It's all
  A trick of the light.

JENNET.   The light of a fire.

THOMAS.   And, Richard,
  Make this woman understand that I
  Am a figure of vice and crime——

JENNET.   Guilty of——

THOMAS.   Guilty
  Of mankind. I have perpetrated human nature.
  My father and mother were accessaries before the fact,
  But there'll be no accessaries after the fact,
  By my virility there won't! Just see me
  As I am, me like a perambulating
  Vegetable, patched with inconsequential
  Hair, looking out of two small jellies for the means
  Of life, balanced on folding bones, my sex
  No beauty but a blemish to be hidden
  Behind judicious rags, driven and scorched
  By boomerang rages and lunacies which never
  Touch the accommodating artichoke
  Or the seraphic strawberry beaming in its bed:
  I defend myself against pain and death by pain
  And death, and make the world go round, they tell me,
  By one of my less lethal appetites:
  Half this grotesque life I spend in a state
  Of slow decomposition, using
  The name of unconsidered God as a pedestal
  On which I stand and bray that I'm best
  Of beasts, until under some patient
  Moon or other I fall to pieces, like

A cake of dung. Is there a slut would hold
This in her arms and put her lips against it?

JENNET. Sluts are only human. By a quirk
Of unastonished nature, your obscene
Decaying figure of vegetable fun
Can drag upon a woman's heart, as though
Heaven were dragging up the roots of hell.
What is to be done? Something compels us into
The terrible fallacy that man is desirable
And there's no escaping into truth. The crimes
And cruelties leave us longing, and campaigning
Love still pitches his tent of light among
The suns and moons. You may be decay and a platitude
Of flesh, but I have no other such memory of life.
You may be corrupt as ancient apples, well then
Corruption is what I most willingly harvest.
You are Evil, Hell, the Father of Lies; if so
Hell is my home and my days of good were a holiday:
Hell is my hill and the world slopes away from it
Into insignificance. I have come suddenly
Upon my heart and where it is I see no help for.

THOMAS. We're lost, both irretrievably lost——

Enter TYSON, TAPPERCOOM, HUMPHREY, *and the* CHAPLAIN.

TAPPERCOOM.   Certainly.
The woman has confessed. *Spargere auras
Per vulgum ambiguas.* The town can go to bed.

TYSON. It was a happy idea, eh, Tappercoom? This will be
A great relief to my sister, and everybody
Concerned. A very nice confession, my dear.

THOMAS. What is this popping-noise? Now what's the matter?

JENNET. Do they think I've confessed to witchcraft?

TAPPERCOOM.   Admirably.

CHAPLAIN [*to* JENNET]. Bother such sadness. You understand,
    I'm sure:
    Those in authority over us. I should like
    To have been a musician but others decreed otherwise.
    And sin, whatever we might prefer, cannot
    Go altogether unregarded.

TAPPERCOOM.   Now,
    Now, Chaplain, don't get out of hand.
    Pieties come later.—Young Devize
    Had better go and calm the populace.
    Tell them faggots will be lit to-morrow at noon.

HUMPHREY. Have a heart, Mr. Tappercoom; they're hurling
    bricks.

JENNET. What do they mean? Am I at noon to go
    To the fire? Oh, for pity! Why must they brand
    Themselves with me?

THOMAS.   She has bribed you to procure
    Her death! Graft! Graft! Oh, the corruption
    Of this town when only the rich can get to kingdom-
    Come and a poor man is left to groan
    In the full possession of his powers. And she's
    Not even guilty! I demand fair play
    For the criminal classes!

TYSON.   Terrible state of mind.
    Humphrey, go at once to the gate——

HUMPHREY.   Ah well, I can
    But try to dodge.

THOMAS [*knocking him down*]. You didn't try soon enough.
    Who else is going to cheat me out of my death?

Whee, ecclesiastic, let me brain you
With your wife!
> [*He snatches the* CHAPLAIN's *viol and offers to hit him on
> the head.*

CHAPLAIN.   No, no! With something else—oh, please
Hit me with something else.

THOMAS.   Exchange it
For a harp and hurry off to heaven.—Am I dangerous?
Will you give me the gallows?—Now, *now*, Mr. Mayor!
Richard, I'll drown him in your bucket.

> [JENNET *faints.*

RICHARD [*running to support her*]. Look, she has fallen!

CHAPLAIN.   Air! Air!

TYSON.   Water!

THOMAS. But no fire, do you hear? No fire!—How is she, Richard?
Oh, the delicate mistiming of women! She has carefully
Snapped in half my jawbone of an ass.

RICHARD. Life is coming back.

THOMAS.   Importunate life.
It should have something better to do
Than to hang about at a chronic street-corner
In dirty weather and worse company.

TAPPERCOOM. It is my duty as Justice to deliver
Sentence on you as well.

THOMAS.   Ah!

TAPPERCOOM.   Found guilty
Of jaundice, misanthropy, suicidal tendencies
And spreading gloom and despondency. You will spend
The evening joyously, sociably, taking part
In the pleasures of your fellow men.

THOMAS.   Not
  Until you've hanged me. I'll be amenable then.

JENNET. Have I come back to consciousness to hear
  That still?—Richard, help me to stand.—You see,
  Preacher to the caddis-fly, I return
  To live my allotted span of insect hours.
  But if you batter my wings with talk of death
  I'll drop to the ground again.

THOMAS.   Ah! One
  Concession to your courage and then no more.
  Gentlemen, I'll accept your most inhuman
  Sentence. I'll not disturb the indolence
  Of your gallows yet. But on one condition:
  That this lady shall take her share to-night
  Of awful festivity. She shall suffer too.

TYSON. Out of the question, quite out of the question,
  Absolutely out of the question. What, what?

TAPPERCOOM. What?

THOMAS.   Then you shall spend your night in searching
  For the bodies of my victims, or else the Lord
  Chief Justice of England shall know you let a murderer
  Go free. I'll raise the country.

JENNET.   Do you think
  I can go in gaiety to-night
  Under the threat of to-morrow? If I could sleep——

THOMAS. That is the heaven to come.
  We should be like stars now that it's dark:
  Use ourselves up to the last bright dregs
  And vanish in the morning. Shall we not
  Suffer as wittily as we can? Now, come,
  Don't purse your lips like a little prude at the humour

Of annihilation. It is somewhat broad
I admit, but we're not children.

JENNET.   I am such
A girl of habit. I had got into the way
Of being alive. I will live as well as I can
This evening.

THOMAS.   And I'll live too, if it kills me.

HUMPHREY. Well, uncle? If you're going to let this clumsy-
Fisted cut-throat loose on the house to-night,
Why not the witch-girl, too?

CHAPLAIN.   Foolishly
I can't help saying it, I should like
To see them dancing.

TYSON. We have reached a decision.
The circumstances compel us to agree
To your most unorthodox request.

THOMAS.   Wisdom
At last. But listen, woman: after this evening
I have no further interest in the world.

JENNET. My interest also will not be great, I imagine,
After this evening.

CURTAIN ON ACT TWO

ACT THREE

Later the same night. The same room, by torchlight and moonlight.
HUMPHREY *at the window. Enter* THOMAS, *who talks to himself*
until he notices HUMPHREY.

THOMAS. O tedium, tedium, tedium. The frenzied
Ceremonial drumming of the humdrum!
Where in this small-talking world can I find
A longitude with no platitude?—I must
Apologize. That was no joke to be heard
Making to myself in the full face of the moon.
If only I had been born flame, a flame
Poised, say, on the flighty head of a candle,
I could have stood in this draught and gone out,
Whip, through the door of my exasperation.
But I remain, like the possibility
Of water in a desert.

HUMPHREY.   I'm sure nobody
Keeps you here. There's a road outside if you want it.

THOMAS. What on earth should I do with a road, that furrow
On the forehead of imbecility, a road?
I would as soon be up there, walking in the moon's
White unmolared gums. I'll sit on the world
And rotate with you till we roll into the morning.

HUMPHREY. You're a pestering parasite. If I had my way
You'd be got rid of. You're mad and you're violent,
And I strongly resent finding you slightly pleasant.

THOMAS. O God, yes, so do I.

Enter NICHOLAS.

NICHOLAS.   As things turn out
I want to commit an offence.

THOMAS.   Does something prevent you?

NICHOLAS. I don't know what offence to commit.

THOMAS.   What abysmal
Poverty of mind!

NICHOLAS.   This is a night
Of the most asphyxiating enjoyment that ever
Sapped my youth.

HUMPHREY.   I think I remember
The stars gave you certain rights and interest
In a little blonde religious. How is she, Nicholas?

NICHOLAS. Your future wife, Humphrey, if that is who
You mean, is pale, tearful, and nibbling a walnut.
I loved her once—earlier to-day—
Loved her with a passionate misapprehension.
I thought you wanted her, and I'm always deeply
Devoted to your affairs. But now I'm bored,
As bored as the face of a fish,
In spite of the sunlit barley of her hair.

HUMPHREY. Aren't I ready to marry her? I thought that was why
We were mooning around celebrating. What more
Can I do to make you take her off my hands?
And I'm more than ready for the Last Trump as well.
It will stop old Mrs. Cartwright talking.

NICHOLAS.   Never.
She's doom itself. She could talk a tombstone off anybody.

Enter MARGARET.

MARGARET. Oh, there you are. Whatever's wrong? You both
Go wandering off, as though our guests could be gay

Of their own accord (the few who could bring themselves
To bring themselves, practically in the teeth
Of the recording angel). They're very nervous
And need considerable jollying. Goose liver,
Cold larks, cranberry tarts and sucking pig,
And now everyone looks as though they only
Wanted to eat each other, which might in the circumstances
Be the best possible thing. Your uncle sent me
To find you. I can tell he's put out; he's as vexed
As a hen's hind feathers in a wind. And for that
Matter so am I. Go back inside
And be jolly like anyone else's children.

NICHOLAS.   Mother,
I'd as soon kiss the bottom of a Barbary ape.
The faces of our friends may be enchantment
To some, but they wrap my spirits in a shroud.—
For the sake of my unborn children, I have to avoid them.
Oh now, be brave, mother. They'll go in the course of nature.

MARGARET. It's unfortunate, considering the wide
Choice of living matter on this globe,
That I should have managed to be a mother. I can't
Imagine what I was thinking of. Your uncle
Has made me shake out the lavender
From one of my first gowns which has hung in the wardrobe
Four-and-twenty unencouraging years,
To lend to this Jennet girl, who in my opinion
Should not be here. And I said to her flatly
'The course of events is incredible. Make free
'With my jewel box.' Where is she now?

THOMAS.   No doubt
Still making free. Off she has gone,
Away to the melting moody horizons of opal,

Moonstone, bloodstone; now moving in lazy
Amber, now sheltering in the shade
Of jade from a brief rainfall of diamonds.
Able to think to-morrow has an even
Brighter air, a glitter less moderate,
A quite unparalleled freedom in the fire:
A death, no bounds to it. Where is she now?
She is dressing, I imagine.

MARGARET.   Yes, I suppose so.
I don't like to think of her. And as for you
I should like to think of you as someone I knew
Many years ago, and, alas, wouldn't see again.
That would be charming. I beg you to come,
Humphrey. Give your brother a good example.

HUMPHREY. Mother, I'm unwell.

MARGARET.   Oh, Humphrey!

NICHOLAS.   Mother,
He is officially sick and actually bored.
The two together are as bad as a dropsy.

MARGARET. I must keep my mind as concentrated as possible
On such pleasant things as the summer I spent at Stoke
D'Abernon. Your uncle must do what he will.
I've done what I can.

                                    [*Exit* MARGARET.

NICHOLAS.   Our mother isn't
Pleased.

HUMPHREY. She has never learnt to yawn
And so she hasn't the smallest comprehension
Of those who can.

THOMAS.   Benighted brothers in boredom,
Let us unite ourselves in a toast of ennui.

I give you a yawn: to this evening, especially remembering
Mrs. Cartwright. [*They all yawn.*] To mortal life, women,
All government, wars, art, science, ambitions,
And the entire fallacy of human emotions!

> [*As they painfully yawn again, enter* JENNET, *bright with
> jewels, and twenty years exquisitely out of fashion.*

JENNET. And wake us in the morning with an ambrosial
Breakfast, amen, amen.

NICHOLAS.   Humphrey, poppin,
Draw back the curtains. I have a sense of daylight.

HUMPHREY. It seems we're facing east.

THOMAS.   You've come too late.
Romulus, Remus and I have just buried the world
Under a heavy snowfall of disinterest.
There's nothing left of life but cranberry tarts,
Goose's liver, sucking pig, cold larks,
And Mrs. Cartwright.

JENNET.   That's riches running mad.
What about the have-not moon? Not a goose, not a pig,
And yet she manages to be the wit
Of heaven, and roused the envious Queen of Sheba
To wash in mercury so that the Sheban fountains
Should splash deliriously in the light of her breast.
But she died, poor Queen, shining less
Than the milk of her thousand shorthorn cows.

THOMAS.   What's this?
Where has the girl I spoke to this evening gone
With her Essential Fact? Surely she knows,
If she is true to herself, the moon is nothing
But a circumambulating aphrodisiac
Divinely subsidized to provoke the world

Into a rising birth-rate—a veneer
Of sheerest Venus on the planks of Time
Which may fool the ocean but which fools not me.

JENNET. So no moon.

THOMAS.   No moon.

NICHOLAS.   Let her have the last quarter.

JENNET.   No;
If he says no moon then of course there can be no moon.
Otherwise we destroy his system of thought
And confuse the quest for truth.

THOMAS.   You see, Nicholas?

JENNET. I've only one small silver night to spend
So show me no luxuries. It will be enough
If you spare me a spider, and when it spins I'll see
The six days of Creation in a web
And a fly caught on the seventh. And if the dew
Should rise in the web, I may well die a Christian.

THOMAS. I must shorten my sail. We're into a strange wind.
This evening you insisted on what you see,
What you touch, what you know. Where did this weather blow
    from?

JENNET. Off the moors of mortality: that might
Be so. Or there's that inland sea, the heart—
But you mustn't hinder me, not now. I come
Of a long-lived family, and I have
Some sixty years to use up almost immediately.
I shall join the sucking pig.

NICHOLAS.   Please take my arm.
I'll guide you there.

HUMPHREY.   He shall do no such thing.
Who's the host here?

THOMAS.   They have impeccable manners
  When they reach a certain temperature.

HUMPHREY.   A word
  More from you, and you go out of this house.

THOMAS. Like the heart going out of me, by which it avoids
  Having to break.

JENNET.   Be quiet for a moment. I hear
  A gay modulating anguish, rather like music.

NICHOLAS. It's the Chaplain, extorting lightness of heart
  From the guts of his viol, to the greater glory of God.

                  Enter HEBBLE TYSON.

TYSON. What I hear from your mother isn't agreeable to me
  In the smallest—a draught, quite noticeable.
  I'm a victim to air.—I expect members of my family——

THOMAS. Is this courtesy, Mr. Mayor, to turn your back
  On a guest?

JENNET.   Why should I be welcome? I am wearing
  His days gone by. I rustle with his memories!
  I, the little heretic as he thinks,
  The all unhallows Eve to his poor Adam;
  And nearly stubbing my toes against my grave
  In his sister's shoes, the grave he has ordered for me.
  Don't ask impossibilities of the gentleman.

TYSON. Humphrey, will you explain yourself?

HUMPHREY.   Uncle,
  I came to cool my brow. I was on my way back.

NICHOLAS. Don't keep us talking. I need to plunge again
  Into that ice-cap of pleasure in the next room.
  I repeat, my arm.

HUMPHREY.   I repeat that I'm the host.
I have the right——

JENNET.   He has the right, Nicholas.
Let me commit no solecism so near
To eternity. Please open the door for us.
We must go in as smoothly as old friends.

[*Exeunt* JENNET, HUMPHREY, *and* NICHOLAS.

THOMAS. Well, does your blood run deep enough to run
Cold, or have you none?

TYSON.   That's enough. Get away.

THOMAS. Are you going to cry-off the burning?

TYSON.   Worthless creatures,
Both; I call you clutter. The standard soul
Must mercilessly be maintained. No
Two ways of life. One God, one point of view.
A general acquiescence to the mean.

THOMAS. And God knows when you say the mean, you mean
The mean. You'd be surprised to see the number
Of cloven hoof-marks in the yellow snow of your soul.
And so you'll kill her.
Time would have done it for her too, of course,
But more cautiously, and with a pretence of charm.
Am I allowed on bail into your garden?

TYSON. Tiresome catarrh. I haven't any wish to see you,
Not in the slightest degree: go where you like.

THOMAS. That's nowhere in this world. But still maybe
I can make myself useful and catch mice for an owl.

[*Exit* THOMAS.

Enter TAPPERCOOM.

TAPPERCOOM. The young lunatic slipping off, is he?
   Cheered up and gone? So much the less trouble for us.
   Very jolly evening, Tyson. Are you sober?

TYSON. Yes, yes, yes.

TAPPERCOOM.   You shouldn't say that, you know.
   You're in tears, Tyson. I know tears when I see them,
   My wife has them. You've drunk too deep, my boy.
   Now I'm sober as a judge, perhaps a judge
   A little on circuit, but still sober. Tyson,
   You're in tears, old fellow, two little wandering
   Jews of tears getting 'emselves embrangled
   In your beard.

TYSON.   I won't stand it, Tappercoom:
   I won't have it, I won't have evil things
   Looking so distinguished. I'm no longer
   Young, and I should be given protection.

TAPPERCOOM.   What
   Do you want protecting from now?

TYSON.   We must burn her,
   Before she destroys our reason. Damnable glitter.
   Tappercoom, we musn't become bewildered
   At our time of life. Too unusual
   Not to be corrupt. Must be burnt
   Immediately, burnt, burnt, Tappercoom,
   Immediately.

TAPPERCOOM. Are you trying to get rid of temptation,
   Tyson? A belated visit of the wanton flesh
   After all these years? You've got to be dispassionate.
   Calm and civilized. I am civilized.
   I know, frinstance, that Beauty is not an Absolute.
   Beauty is a Condition. As you might say

                                             G

Hey nonny no or Hey nonny yes.
But the Law's about as absolute an Absolute—
Hello, feeling dicky, Chaplain?

> [*The* CHAPLAIN *has entered, crying.*

CHAPLAIN.   It would be
So kind if you didn't notice me. I have
Upset myself. I have no right to exist,
Not in any form, I think.

TAPPERCOOM.   I hope you won't
Think me unsociable if I don't cry myself.
What's the matter? Here's the pair of you
Dripping like newly weighed anchors.
Let the butterflies come to you, Chaplain,
Or you'll never be pollinated into a Bishop.

CHAPLAIN. No, it's right and it's just I should be cast down.
I've treated her with an abomination
That maketh desolate:—the words, the words
Are from Daniel——

TAPPERCOOM.   Hey, what's this? The young woman again?

CHAPLAIN. My patient instrument. I made my viol
Commit such sins of sound—and I didn't mind:
No, I laughed. I was trying to play a dance.
I'm too unaccomplished to play with any jollity.
I shouldn't venture beyond religious pieces.

TYSON. There's no question of jollity. We've got
To burn her, for our peace of mind.

TAPPERCOOM.   You must wait
Until to-morrow, like a reasonable chap.
And to-morrow, remember, you'll have her property
Instead of your present longing for impropriety.
And her house, now I come to think of it,

Will suit me nicely.
A large mug of small beer for both of you.
Leave it to me.

CHAPLAIN.   No, no, no,
I should become delighted again. I wish
For repentance——

                    Enter RICHARD.

TAPPERCOOM.   You shall have it. I'll pour it out
Myself. You'll see: it shall bring you to your knees.

CHAPLAIN. I'm too unaccomplished. I haven't the talent,
But I hoped I should see them dancing. And after all
They didn't dance——

TAPPERCOOM.   They shall, dear saint, they shall.

                    [*Exit* TAPPERCOOM *and the* CHAPLAIN.

RICHARD. I was to tell you, Mr. Tyson——

TYSON.   I'm not
To be found. I'm fully occupied elsewhere.
If you wish to find me I shall be in my study.
You can knock, but I shall give you no reply.
I wish to be alone with my own convictions.
Good-night.

                    [*Exit* TYSON. THOMAS *looks through the window.*

                    Enter ALIZON.

THOMAS [*to* RICHARD]. The Great Bear is looking so geometrical
One would think that something or other could be proved.
Are you sad, Richard?

RICHARD.   Certainly.

THOMAS.   I also.
I've been cast adrift on a raft of melancholy.
The night-wind passed me, like a sail across
A blind man's eye. There it is,

The interminable tumbling of the great grey
Main of moonlight, washing over
The little oyster-shell of this month of April:
Among the raven-quills of the shadows
And on the white pillows of men asleep:
The night's a boundless pastureland of peace,
And something condones the world, incorrigibly.
But what, in fact, *is* this vaporous charm?
We're softened by a nice conglomeration
Of the earth's uneven surface, refraction of light,
Obstruction of light, condensation, distance,
And that sappy upshot of self-centred vegetablism
The trees of the garden. How is it we come
To see this as a heaven in the eye?
Why should we hawk and spit out ecstasy
As though we were nightingales, and call these quite
Casual degrees and differences
Beauty? What guile recommends the world
And gives our eyes the special sense to be
Deluded, above all animals?—Stone me, Richard!
I've begun to talk like that soulless girl, and she
May at this moment be talking like me! I shall go
Back into the garden, and choke myself with the seven
Sobs I managed to bring with me from the wreck.

RICHARD. To hear her you would think her feet had almost
Left the ground. The evening which began
So blackly, now, as though it were a kettle
Set over her flame, has started to sing. And all
The time I find myself praying under my breath
That something will save her.

THOMAS.   You might do worse.
Tides turn with a similar sort of whisper.

ALIZON. Richard.

RICHARD.   Alizon!

ALIZON.   I've come to be with you.

RICHARD. Not with me. I'm the to-and-fro fellow
To-night. You have to be with Humphrey.

ALIZON.   I think
I have never met Humphrey. I have met him less
And less the more I have seen him.

THOMAS.   You will forgive me.
I was mousing for a small Dutch owl.
If it has said towoo t-wice it has said it
A thousand times.

                          [*He disappears into the garden.*

RICHARD.   Hey! Thomas—! Ah well.—
The crickets are singing well with their legs to night.

ALIZON. It sounds as though the night-air is riding
On a creaking saddle.

RICHARD.   You must go back to the others.

ALIZON. Let me stay. I'm not able to love them.
Have you forgotten what they mean to do
To-morrow?

RICHARD.   How could I forget? But there are laws
And if someone fails them——

ALIZON.   I shall run
Away from laws if laws can't live in the heart.
I shall be gone to-morrow.

RICHARD.   You make the room
Suddenly cold. Where will you go?

ALIZON.   Where
Will you come to find me?

RICHARD.   Look, you've pulled the thread
In your sleeve. Is it honest for me to believe
You would be unhappy?

ALIZON.   When?

RICHARD.   If you marry Humphrey?

ALIZON. Humphrey's a winter in my head.
But whenever my thoughts are cold and I lay them
Against Richard's name, they seem to rest
On the warm ground where summer sits
As golden as a humblebee.
So I did very little but think of you
Until I ran out of the room.

RICHARD.   Do you come to me
Because you can never love the others?

ALIZON.   Our father
God moved many lives to show you to me.
I think that is the way it must have happened.
It was complicated, but very kind.

RICHARD.   If I asked you
If you could ever love me, I should know
For certain that I was no longer rational.

ALIZON. I love you quite as much as I love St. Anthony
And rather more than I love St. John Chrysostom.

RICHARD. But putting haloes on one side, as a man
Could you love me, Alizon?

ALIZON.   I have become
A woman, Richard, because I love you. I know
I was a child three hours ago. And yet
I love you as deeply as many years could make me,
But less deeply than many years will make me.

RICHARD. I think I may never speak steadily again.
What have I done or said to make it possible
That you should love me?

ALIZON.   Everything I loved
Before has come to one meeting place in you
And you have gone out into everything I love.

RICHARD. Happiness seems to be weeping in me, as
I suppose it should, being newly born.

ALIZON. We must never leave each other now, or else
We should perplex the kindness of God.   .

RICHARD.   The kindness
Of God in itself is not a little perplexing.
What do we do?

ALIZON.   We cleave to each other, Richard.
That is what is proper for us to do.

RICHARD. But you were promised to Humphrey, Alizon.
And I'm hardly more than a servant here
Tied to my own apron-strings. They'll never
Let us love each other.

ALIZON.   Then they will have
To outwit all that ever went to create us.

RICHARD. So they will. I believe it. Let them storm.
We're lovers in a deep and safe place
And never lonely any more.—Alizon,
Shall we make the future, however much it roars,
Lie down with our happiness? Are you ready
To forgo custom and escape with me?

ALIZON. Shall we go now, before anyone prevents us?

RICHARD. I'll take you to the old priest who first found me.
He is as near to being my father

As putting his hand into a poor-box could make him.
He'll help us. Oh, Alizon, I so
Love you. Let yourself quietly out and wait for me
Somewhere near the gate but in a shadow.
I must fetch my savings. Are you afraid?

ALIZON.   In some
Part of me, not all; and while I wait
I can have a word with the saints Theresa and Christopher:
They may have some suggestions.

RICHARD.   Yes, do that.
Now: like a mouse.

                    [When she has gone he goes to the window.
                    Only let me spell
No disillusion for her, safety, peace,
And a good world, as good as she has made it!

                              *[*RICHARD *starts to fetch his money.*

                    Enter MARGARET.

MARGARET. Now, Richard: have you found Mr. Tyson?

RICHARD.   Yes;
He's busy with his convictions.

MARGARET.   He has no business
To be busy now. How am I to prevent
This girl, condemned as a heretic, from charming us
With gentleness, consideration and gaiety?
It makes orthodoxy seem almost irrelevant.
But I expect they would tell us the soul can be as lost
In loving-kindness as in anything else.
Well, well; we must scramble for grace as best we can.
Where is Alizon?

RICHARD.   I must—I must——

MARGARET. The poor child has gone away to cry.
See if you can find her, will you, Richard?

RICHARD. I have to—have to——

MARGARET. Very well. I will go
In search of the sad little soul myself.
Oh dear, I could do with a splendid holiday
In a complete vacuum.

[*Exit* MARGARET *one way*, RICHARD, *hastily, another.*

Enter JENNET. *She seems for a moment exhausted, but crosses to the
window. Enter* NICHOLAS *and* HUMPHREY.

NICHOLAS. Are you tired of us?

HUMPHREY. Why on earth
Can't you stop following her?

NICHOLAS. Stop following me.

JENNET. I am troubled to find Thomas Mendip.

NICHOLAS. He's far gone—
As mad as the nature of man.

HUMPHREY. As rude and crude
As an act of God. He'll burn your house.

JENNET. So he has.—
Are you kind to mention burning?

HUMPHREY I beg your pardon.

NICHOLAS. Couldn't you to-morrow by some elementary spell
Reverse the direction of the flames and make them burn down-
wards?
It would save you unpleasantness and increase at the same
Time the heat below, which would please
Equally heaven and hell.
I feel such a tenderness for you, not only because
I think you've bewitched my brother, which would be

A most salutary thing, but because, even more
Than other women, you carry a sense of that cavernous
Night folded in night, where Creation sleeps
And dreams of men. If only we loved each other
Down the pitshaft of love I could go
To the motive mysteries under the soul's floor.
Well drenched in damnation I should be as pure
As a limewashed wall.

HUMPHREY.   Get out!

JENNET.   He does no harm.—
Is it possible he still might make for death
Even on this open-hearted night?

HUMPHREY.   Who might?

JENNET. Thomas Mendip. He's sick of the world, but the world
Has a right to him.

HUMPHREY.   Damn Thomas Mendip.

NICHOLAS.   Nothing
Easier.
          Enter RICHARD, *upset to see his escape cut off.*

          You're just the fellow, Richard:
We need some more Canary, say five bottles
More. And before we go in, we'll drink here, privately,
To beauty and the sombre sultry waters
Where beauty haunts.

RICHARD.   I have to find—to find——

NICHOLAS. Five bottles of Canary. I'll come to the cellars
And help you bring them. Quick, before our mother
Calls us back to evaporate into duty.

                    [*Exit* NICHOLAS, *taking* RICHARD *with him.*

HUMPHREY. He's right. You have bewitched me. But not by
      brews
   And incantations. For all I know
   You may have had some traffic with the Devil
   And made some sinister agreement with him
   To your soul's cost. If so, you will agree
   The fire is fair, as fair goes:
   You have to burn.

JENNET.   It's hard enough to live
   These last few hours as the earth deserves.
   Do you have to remind me how soon the night
   Will leave me unprotected, at the daylight's mercy?
   I'm tired, trying to fight those thoughts away.

HUMPHREY. But need you? These few hours of the night
   Might be lived in a way which wouldn't end
   In fire. It would be insufferable
   If you were burned before I could know you.
   I should never sit at ease in my body again.

JENNET. Must we talk of this? All there is
   To be said has been said, and all in a heavy sentence.
   There's nothing to add, except a grave silence.

HUMPHREY. Listen, will you listen? There is more to say.
   I'm able to save you, since all official action
   Can be given official hesitation. I happen
   To be on the Council, and a dozen reasons
   Can be found to postpone the moment of execution:
   Legal reasons, monetary reasons—
   They've confiscated your property, and I can question
   Whether your affairs may not be too disordered.
   And once postponed, a great congestion of quibbles
   Can be let loose over the Council table——

JENNET. Hope can break the heart, Humphrey. Hope
Can be too strong.

HUMPHREY.   But this is true: actual
As my body is. And as for that—now, impartially,
Look what I risk. If in fact you have
Done anything to undermine our fairly
Workable righteousness, and they say you have,
Then my status in both this town and the after-life
Will be gone if either suspect me of having helped you.
I have to be given a considerable reason
For risking that.

JENNET.   I fondly hope I'm beginning
To misconstrue you.

HUMPHREY.   Later on to-night
When they're all bedded-down in their beauty-sleep
I'll procure the key and come to your cell. Is that
Agreeable?

JENNET.   Is it so to you?
Aren't you building your castles in foul air?

HUMPHREY. Foul? No; it's give and take, the basis
Of all understanding.

JENNET.   You mean you give me a choice:
To sleep with you, or to-morrow to sleep with my fathers.
And if I value the gift of life,
Which, dear heaven, I do, I can scarcely refuse.

HUMPHREY. Isn't that sense?

JENNET.   Admirable sense.
Oh, why, why am I not sensible?
Oddly enough, I hesitate. Can I
So dislike being cornered by a young lecher
That I should rather die? That would be

The maniac pitch of pride. Indeed, it might
Even be sin. Can I believe my ears?
I seem to be considering heaven. And heaven,
From this angle, seems considerable.

HUMPHREY. Now, please, we're not going to confuse the soul and
    the body.
This, speaking bodily, is merely an exchange
Of compliments.

JENNET.   And surely throwing away
My life for the sake of pride would seem to heaven
A bodily blasphemy, a suicide?

HUMPHREY. Even if heaven were interested. Or even
If you cared for heaven. Am I unattractive to you?

JENNET. Except that you have the manners of a sparrowhawk,
With less reason, no, you are not. But even so
I no more run to your arms than I wish to run
To death. I ask myself why. Surely I'm not
Mesmerized by some snake of chastity?

HUMPHREY. This isn't the time——

JENNET.   Don't speak, contemptible boy,
I'll tell you: I am not. We have
To look elsewhere—for instance, into my heart
Where recently I heard begin
A bell of longing which calls no one to church.
But need that, ringing anyway in vain,
Drown the milkmaid singing in my blood
And freeze into the tolling of my knell?
That would be pretty, indeed, but unproductive.
No, it's not that.

HUMPHREY.   Jennet, before they come
And interrupt us——

JENNET.   I am interested
   In my feelings. I seem to wish to have some importance
   In the play of time. If not,
   Then sad was my mother's pain, my breath, my bones,
   My web of nerves, my wondering brain,
   To be shaped and quickened with such anticipation
   Only to feed the swamp of space.
   What is deep, as love is deep, I'll have
   Deeply. What is good, as love is good,
   I'll have well. Then if time and space
   Have any purpose, I shall belong to it.
   If not, if all is a pretty fiction
   To distract the cherubim and seraphim
   Who so continually do cry, the least
   I can do is to fill the curled shell of the world
   With human deep-sea sound, and hold it to
   The ear of God, until he has appetite
   To taste our salt sorrow on his lips.
   And so you see it might be better to die.
   Though, on the other hand, I admit it might
   Be immensely foolish.—Listen! What
   Can all that thundering from the cellars be?

HUMPHREY. I don't know at all. You're simply playing for time.
   Why can't you answer me, before I'm thrown
   By the bucking of my pulse, before Nicholas
   Interrupts us? Will it be all right?

JENNET. Doesn't my plight seem pitiable to you?

HUMPHREY. Pitiable, yes. It makes me long for you
   Intolerably. Now, be a saint, and tell me
   I may come to your cell.

JENNET.   I wish I could believe

My freedom was not in the flames. O God, I wish
The ground would open.

                    [THOMAS *climbs in through the window.*

THOMAS.   Allow me to open it for you.
Admit I was right. Man's a mistake.
Lug-worms, the lot of us.

HUMPHREY.   Wipe your filthy boots
Before you start trespassing.

THOMAS.   And as for you
I'll make you the climax to my murders.
You can die a martyr to the cause
Of bureaucratic pollution.

JENNET.   Oh dear,
Is this lug-worms at war? And by what right, will you tell me,
Do you come moralizing in, dictating
What I should do?

THOMAS.   Woman, what are you saying?
Are you trying to tell me you'd even consider——

JENNET. I might prefer the dragon to St. George.

HUMPHREY. If he wants to fight me, let him. Come out into the
    garden.
If he kills me
Remember I thought you unfairly beautiful
And, to balance your sins, you should be encouraged
To spend your beauty in a proper way,
On someone who knows its worth.

THOMAS. Sound the trumpets!

JENNET.   Yes, why not? And a roll

Of drums. You, if you remember, failed
Even to give me a choice. You have only said
'Die, woman, and look as though you liked it.'
So you'll agree this can hardly be said to concern you.

THOMAS. All right! You've done your worst. You force me to
　　tell you
The disastrous truth. I love you. A misadventure
So intolerable, hell could not do more.
Nothing in the world could touch me
And you have to come and be the damnable
Exception. I was nicely tucked up for the night
Of eternity, and, like a restless dream
Of a fool's paradise, you, with a rainbow where
Your face is and an *ignis fatuus*
Worn like a rose in your girdle, come pursued
By fire, and presto! the bedclothes are on the floor
And I, the tomfool, love you. Don't say again
That this doesn't concern me, or I shall say
That you needn't concern yourself with to-morrow's burning.
　　　　　　　　　Enter NICHOLAS.

NICHOLAS. Do you know what that little bastard Richard did?
He locked me in the cellars.

THOMAS.　　　　　　　　　　Don't complicate
The situation.—I love you, perfectly knowing
You're nothing but a word out of the mouth
Of that same planet of almighty blemish
Which I long to leave. But the word so sings
With an empty promise.—I shall lie in my grave
With my hands clapped over my ears, to stop your music
From riddling me as much as the meddling worms.
Still, that's beside the point. We have to settle
This other matter——

NICHOLAS.   Yes, I was telling you.
  I went into the cellars to get the wine,
  And the door swung after me, and that little son
  Of a crossbow turned the key——

THOMAS [*to* JENNET].   Can we find somewhere
  To talk where there isn't quite so much insect life?

NICHOLAS. And there I was, in cobwebs up to my armpits,
  Hammering the door and yelling like a slaughter-house,
  Until the cook came and let me out. Where is he?

JENNET. What should we talk of? You mean to be hanged.
  Am I to understand that your tongue-tied dust
  Will slip a ring on the finger of my ashes
  And we'll both die happily ever after? Surely
  The other suggestion, though more conventional,
  Has fewer flaws?

THOMAS.   But you said, like a ray of truth
  Itself, that you'd rather burn.

JENNET.   My heart, my mind
  Would rather burn. But may not the casting vote
  Be with my body? And is the body necessarily
  Always ill-advised?

NICHOLAS.   Something has happened
  Since I made the descent into those hellish cobwebs.
  I'm adrift. What is it?

THOMAS.   Let me speak to her.
  You've destroyed my defences, the laborious contrivance
  Of hours, the precious pair of you. O Jennet,
  Jennet, you should have let me go, before
  I confessed a word of this damned word love. I'll not
  Reconcile myself to a dark world
  For the sake of five-feet six of wavering light,

For the sake of a woman who goes no higher
Than my bottom lip.

NICHOLAS.   I'll strip and fly my shirt
At the masthead unless someone picks me up.
What has been going on?

THOMAS.   Ask that neighing
Horse-box-kicker there, your matchless brother.

NICHOLAS. Ah, Humphrey darling, have there been
Some official natural instincts?

HUMPHREY.   I've had enough.
The whole thing's become unrecognizable.

JENNET [*to* THOMAS]. Have I a too uncertain virtue to keep you
On the earth?

THOMAS.   I ask nothing, nothing. Stop
Barracking my heart. Save yourself
His way if you must. There will always be
Your moment of hesitation, which I shall chalk
All over the walls of purgatory. Never mind
That, loving you, I've trodden the garden threadbare
Completing a way to save you.

JENNET.   If you saved me
Without wishing to save yourself, you might have saved
Your trouble.

NICHOLAS.   I imagine it's all over with us, Humphrey.
I shall go and lie with my own thoughts
And conceive reciprocity. Come on, you boy of gloom.
The high seas for us.

HUMPHREY.   Oh go and drown yourself
And me with you.

NICHOLAS.   There's no need to drown.
We'll take the tails off mermaids.

Enter MARGARET.

MARGARET.   Have any of you
Seen that poor child Alizon? I think
She must be lost.

NICHOLAS.   Who isn't? The best
Thing we can do is to make wherever we're lost in
Look as much like home as we can. Now don't
Be worried. She can't be more lost than she was with us.

HUMPHREY. I can't marry her, mother. Could you think
Of something else to do with her?
I'm going to bed.

NICHOLAS.   I think Humphrey has been
Improperly making a proper suggestion, mother.
He wishes to be drowned.

MARGARET [*to* THOMAS].   They find it impossible
To concentrate. Have you seen the little
Fair-haired girl?

NICHOLAS.   He wishes to be hanged.

MARGARET [*to* JENNET]. Have you hidden the child?

NICHOLAS.   She wishes to be burned
Rather than sleep with my brother.

MARGARET.   She should be thankful
She can sleep at all. For years I have woken up
Every quarter of an hour. I must sit down.
I'm too tired to know what anyone's saying.

JENNET. I think none of us knows where to look for Alizon.
Or for anything else. But shall we, while we wait
For news of her, as two dispirited women
Ask this man to admit he did no murders?

THOMAS. You think not?

JENNET.   I know. There was a soldier,
Discharged and centreless, with a towering pride
In his sensibility, and an endearing
Disposition to be a hero, who wanted
To make an example of himself to all
Erring mankind, and falling in with a witch-hunt
His good heart took the opportunity
Of providing a diversion. O Thomas,
It was very theatrical of you to choose the gallows.

THOMAS. Mother, we won't listen to this girl.
She is jealous, because of my intimate relations
With damnation. But damnation knows
I love her.

RICHARD [*appearing in the doorway*]. We have come back.

NICHOLAS. I want to talk to you. Who locked me in the cellars?

MARGARET [*as* ALIZON *enters*]. Alizon, where have you been?

ALIZON.   We had to come back.

MARGARET. Back? From where?

RICHARD.   We came across old Skipps.

ALIZON. We were running away. We wanted to be happy.

NICHOLAS. Skipps?

HUMPHREY.   The body of old Skipps? We'd better
Find Tappercoom.

                                        [*Exit* HUMPHREY.

MARGARET.   Alizon, what do you mean,
Running away?

RICHARD.   He is rather drunk. Shall I bring him
In? He had been to see his daughter.

JENNET [*to* THOMAS].   Who
  Will trouble to hang you now?   [*She goes up the stairs.*

THOMAS [*calling after her*]. He couldn't lie quiet
  Among so many bones. He had to come back
  To fetch his barrow.

TAPPERCOOM [*entering with* HUMPHREY]. What's all this I'm told?
  I was hoping to hang on my bough for the rest of the evening
  Ripe and undisturbed. What is it? Murder
  Not such a fabrication after all?

ALIZON. We had to come back, you see, because nobody now
  Will be able to burn her.

RICHARD.   Nobody now will be able
  To say she turned him into a dog. Come in,
  Mr. Skipps.

             Enter SKIPPS, *unsteady.*

TAPPERCOOM. It looks uncommonly to me
  As though someone has been tampering with the evidence.
  Where's Tyson? I'm too amiable to-night
  To controvert any course of events whatsoever.

SKIPPS. Your young gentleman says Come in, so I comes in.
  Youse only has to say muck off, and I goes, wivout argument.

TAPPERCOOM. Splendid, of course. Are you the rag-and-bone
  merchant of this town, name of Matthew Skipps?

SKIPPS. Who give me that name? My granfathers and gran-
  mothers and all in authorority undrim. Baptized I blaming was,
  and I says to youse, baptized I am, and I says to youse, baptized
  I will be, wiv holy weeping and washing of teeth. And immer-
  sion upon us miserable offenders. Miserable offenders all—no
  offence meant. And if any of youse is not a miserable offender, as
  he's told to be by almighty and mercerable God, then I says to
  him Hands off my daughter, you bloody-minded heathen.

TAPPERCOOM. All right, all right——

SKIPPS. And I'm not quarrelling, mind; I'm not quarrelling. Peace on earth and good tall women. And give us our trespassers as trespassers will be prosecuted for us. I'm not perfect, mind. But I'm as good a miserable offender as any man here present, ladies excepted.

THOMAS. Here now, Matt, aren't you forgetting yourself? You're dead: you've been dead for hours.

SKIPPS. Dead, am I? I has the respect to ask you to give me coabberation of that. I says mucking liar to nobody. But I seen my daughter three hours back, and she'd have said fair and to my face Dad, you're dead. She don't stand for no nonsense.

NICHOLAS. The whole town knows it, Skipps, old man. You've been dead since this morning.

SKIPPS. Dead. Well, you take my breaf away. Do I begin to stink, then?

HUMPHREY. You do.

SKIPPS. Fair enough. That's coabberation. I'm among the blessed saints.

TAPPERCOOM. He floats in the heaven of the grape. Someone take him home to his hovel.

SKIPPS [*roaring*]. Alleluia! Alleluia! Alleluia!

TAPPERCOOM. Now, stop that, Skipps. Keep your hosannas for the cold light of morning or we shall lock you up.

SKIPPS. Alleluia!

TAPPERCOOM. He'll wake your guests and spoil their pleasure. They're all sitting half sunk in a reef of collars. Even the dear good Chaplain has taken so many glassesful of repentance he's almost unconscious of the existence of sin.

SKIPPS. Glory, amen! Glory, glory, amen, amen!

MARGARET. Richard will take this old man home. Richard—
Where is Richard? Where is Alizon?
Have they gone again?

NICHOLAS.   Yes; Humphrey's future wife,
Blown clean away.

MARGARET.   Yes; that's all very well;
But she mustn't think she can let herself be blown
Away whenever she likes.

THOMAS.   What better time
Than when she likes?

SKIPPS.   As it was in the beginning,
Ever and ever, amen, al-leluia!

MARGARET. Take the old man to his home. Now that you've
made him
Think he's dead we shall never have any peace.

HUMPHREY. Nor shall we when he's gone.

NICHOLAS. Spread your wings, Matthew; we're going to teach
you to fly.

SKIPPS. I has the respect to ask to sit down. Youse blessed saints
Don't realize: it takes it out of you, this life everlasting. Alleluia!

NICHOLAS. ·   Come on.
Your second wind can blow where no one listens.

                    [*Exeunt* HUMPHREY, NICHOLAS, *and* SKIPPS.

TAPPERCOOM. That's more pleasant.
What was the thread, now, which the rascal broke?
Do I have to collect my thoughts any further?

MARGARET.   Yes:
Or I must. That poor child Alizon

Is too young to go throwing herself under the wheels
Of happiness. She should have wrapped up warmly first.
Hebble must know, in any case. I must tell him,
Though he's locked himself in, and only blows his nose
When I knock.

TAPPERCOOM.   Yes, get him on to a horse;
It will do him good.

MARGARET.   Hebble on a horse is a man
Delivered neck and crop to the will of God.
But he'll have to do it.

                              [*Exit* MARGARET.

TAPPERCOOM.   Ah yes, he'll have to do it.
He's a dear little man.—What's to be the end of you?
I take it the male prisoner is sufficiently
Deflated not to plague us with his person
Any longer?

THOMAS.   Deflated? I'm overblown
With the knowledge of my villainy.

TAPPERCOOM.   Your guilt, my boy,
Is a confounded bore.

THOMAS.   Then let it bore me to extinction.

                [JENNET *returns, wearing her own dress.*

TAPPERCOOM. The woman prisoner may notice, without
My mentioning it, that there's a certain mildness
In the night, a kind of somnolent inattention.
If she wishes to return to her cell, no one
Can object. On the other hand—How very empty
The streets must be just now.—You will forgive
A yawn in an overworked and elderly man.—

The moon is full, of course. To leave the town
Unobserved, one would have to use caution. As for me
I shall go and be a burden to my bed.
Good night.

JENNET.   Good night.

THOMAS.   Good night.

> [*Exit* TAPPERCOOM.

THOMAS.   -   So much for me.

JENNET.   Thomas, only another
Fifty years or so and then I promise
To let you go.

THOMAS.   Do you see those roofs and spires?
There sleep hypocrisy, porcous pomposity, greed,
Lust, vulgarity, cruelty, trickery, sham
And all possible nitwittery—are you suggesting fifty
Years of that?

JENNET.   I was only suggesting fifty
Years of me.

THOMAS.   Girl, you haven't changed the world.
Glimmer as you will, the world's not changed.
I love you, but the world's not changed. Perhaps
I could draw you up over my eyes for a time
But the world sickens me still.

JENNET.   And do you think
Your gesture of death is going to change it? Except
For me.

THOMAS. Oh, the unholy mantrap of love!

JENNET. I have put on my own gown again,
But otherwise everything that is familiar,
My house, my poodle, peacock, and possessions,

I have to leave. The world is looking frozen
And forbidding under the moon; but I must be
Out of this town before daylight comes, and somewhere,
Who knows where, begin again.

THOMAS.   Brilliant!
So you fall back on the darkness to defeat me.
You gamble on the possibility
That I was well-brought-up. And, of course, you're right.
I have to see you home, though neither of us
Knows where on earth it is.

JENNET.   Thomas, can you mean to let
The world go on?

THOMAS.   I know my limitations.
When the landscape goes to seed, the wind is obsessed
By to-morrow.

JENNET.   I shall have to hurry.
That was the pickaxe voice of a cock, beginning
To break up the night. Am I an inconvenience
To you?

THOMAS.   As inevitably as original sin.
And I shall be loath to forgo one day of you,
Even for the sake of my ultimate friendly death.

JENNET. I am friendly too.

THOMAS.   Then let me wish us both
Good morning.—And God have mercy on our souls.

THE CURTAIN FALLS